Sandyisms

Stories, Recipes & More
from the North Shore

Sandy Holthaus

authorHOUSE®

AuthorHouse™
1663 Liberty Drive
Bloomington, IN 47403
www.authorhouse.com
Phone: 1-800-839-8640

Published by AuthorHouse 4/5/2012

ISBN: 978-1-4685-6276-7 (e)
ISBN: 978-1-4685-6277-4 (hc)
ISBN: 978-1-4685-6278-1 (sc)

Library of Congress Control Number: 2012904852

Cover Photo courtesy of Linda Lamb of Lamb's Campground
Cover Image: View of Father Baraga's cross from the beach in
Schroeder and a rock cairn, marking my way home.
Cover Art by Amy Miller of Big Woods Design
Editing Support by Katie Bergesch
Author Image by Marguerite
Hair and Make Up by Ann of Diva's

Recommendations

I have been a loyal reader of Sandy Holthaus' column 'Taste of Home' in the Annandale Advocate for many years. Sandy's memories of growing up in Northern Minnesota are heart-warming and humorous. Present day stories of her family life in South Haven, MN with husband Mike, and children Zoë, Ben, and Jack are funny and masterfully written. I am sure readers will find this book a wonderful read and a practical source for some great Minnesota recipes.

Thomas 'Papa Tom' Westman
Southside Township, MN

Sandy Holthaus's recollections of growing up on the North Shore and her hilarious observations on the absurdities of daily life leave me clutching my stomach in pain from laughing so hard. She can make anything funny.

Sandy often makes fun of her own zany idiosyncrasies, but they're heartwarming because they land so close to home. Sometimes she's so poignant she makes me cry. Somehow she weaves every story into recipes that are both delectable and doable.

I eagerly anticipate every word that rolls off Sandy's pen.

Jane Howard
Associate Editor
Cook County News-Herald
Grand Marais, Minnesota

Reader Praise

"Another slam-dunk, Sandy! Very fun and very funny! I tried the turkey recipe. It was fantastic. So easy and so good!"

"I LOVE, LOVE, LOVE your column this week! What a great, fabulous, outrageously wonderful ending!!!! My heart is totally warmed! It brought me to tears."

"Oh, Sandy, you've outdone yourself this time! You are one of the funniest people I've ever met, and you are a fantastic writer!"

Dedication

I dedicate this book to my husband Mike and my three children, Zoë, Jack and Ben. Also to my parents, Art and LaVonne Anderson, my sister-cousin Dawn Sorensen and to anyone who sent prayers and words of encouragement in my direction. You are my "Big Rocks".

I want to thank Linda Lamb for the use of her beautiful photo for the book cover; Steve Prinsen of the Annandale Advocate for the opportunity write for his paper; Rhonda Silence and Jane Howard of the Cook County Star for their humor and support; and Tom Westman for his thoughtful forward. A special thank you to Katie Bergesch for her keen editing eye. And last but never least a thank you to all my neighbors, family and friends who supplied me with all the amazing stories I needed to keep writing this column for so long. Keep them coming, it's not over yet!

I became a columnist by chance but an author by choice. In 2006 I was contemplating my work options. All three of my children, Zoë, Jack and Ben, were all in school but my husband, Mike, was traveling several nights a week for his job. I wanted to do something from home that was both flexible and creative. I made a list of my favorite hobbies and two jumped right to the top, cooking and writing. I started with stories about my childhood on the North Shore of Lake Superior then I would add a couple of recipes from one of my Grandma's recipe boxes. (I happen to have a total of six recipe boxes from my grandmothers, Isabelle Allard and Sara "Marion" Moulton.) I was then published in the Annandale Advocate. Readers liked it and that was that, I became a columnist. Later the Cook County News Herald in Grand Marais and other Minnesota papers ran the column.

Several readers suggested I put them together into a book, (which my friend is what you are now holding in your hands.)

The fact that you are reading this is such a gift to me. In my greatest dreams I never imagined that I would be an author. It was my mother's prodding and support that finally brought this book to a reality and for that I thank her from the depths of my heart. I love you Mom.

I hope you enjoy Sandyisms: Stories, Recipes
& More from the North Shore
Peace to you, Sandy

Forward

View of Grand Marais taken from Rock Cut curve, now known as Cut Face

"We have vainly imagined, in the deceitfulness of our hearts, that all these blessings were produced by some superior wisdom and virtue of our own. Intoxicated with unbroken success, we have become too self-sufficient to feel the necessity of redeeming and preserving grace, too proud to pray to the God that made us." ~ Abraham Lincoln

I am lucky. I was born with a belief that there was something bigger than myself watching over me and protecting me. If I was hurt or sad or scared I could center myself and a feeling of love and peace would wash over me like a warm rain and I would know everything would be all right. When I was old enough to study faith I was taught to believe that this peace was God. I did however, have my doubts that God really existed.

That all changed August 18, 1984.

My first year of college was at the saddest time of my life. I was lonely and afraid, living in the cities away from all family and friends. I started to get sick a lot due to homesickness and stress. I was at a breaking point. It was August and I was on my way to a wedding. Several people from my hometown would be there. I was really excited to go. During the ceremony, I was overcome with anxiety and loneliness because I knew after the weekend was over I would be all alone again. I left mid-ceremony in tears and went to a park. Before long I was on my knees almost hysterical. I prayed to God to help me. I asked that he please send me someone to talk to so I wouldn't feel so alone. Suddenly my tears were dry and I felt at peace for the first time in weeks. It was out of my hands. I had to trust that God would take care of me. I fixed my makeup and returned to the reception. Then it happened. I was barely in the doorway when a woman I hardly knew came up to me, took my hands and said "God told me to talk to you and tell you it will be all right." I was amazed by her words as I had only asked God for exactly this just minutes before. She became my friend, my mentor and my spiritual guide. From that day forward I have never doubted God's existence. This understanding has given me a strength I didn't know I had. My wish is that everyone could have a similar experience. To know deep in my heart there is a God, I find both great comfort and great freedom.

I thank my friend Betty for listening to God's request that August day and giving me the greatest gift of my life. The *absolute certainty* that God is real.

I Enjoy Dessert First
(First Column Published – 2006)

I am really a dessert first kind of person. Some may see this as a character flaw while I see myself as someone who likes to enjoy the great gifts of life on an empty stomach.

I grew up in the great north woods of Minnesota, one mile from the shore of Lake Superior. We were a small family of four, just my parents, my brother and me. My Mom and Dad were in their early 20's when we were born so maybe that's why we enjoyed special treats as kids; because my parents were still "kids" themselves. We didn't have indoor plumbing or running water until I entered kindergarten. We did have electricity though so we could at least see the path to the outhouse.

I grew up with homemade ice cream, made in the winter. I don't ever remember having it in the summer, probably because we would have had to buy or make the ice. In the winter ice was plenty and free. Either we pulled icicles from the house or chopped it from a nearby lake and carried it home in a gunny sack. We'd pack all around the ice cream freezer layers of ice and rock salt. My brother and I would sneak big pieces of rock salt and suck on them like candy while we waited for the ice cream to freeze. We usually made ice cream when we had neighbors or friends visiting, which was often. The best part was the paddle from the middle of the mixer. Mom would lay it on a plate and my brother and I would go at it with spoons until it looked clean enough to skip the dishwater.

Store bought ice cream was a nightly ritual in our house. Mom would bring it home in the 5 quart "Texas Gallon" pails and we ate it at bedtime, if we were good. If we got to fighting we would be sent to bed without ice cream. Dad would still have his treat though and scrapped the metal spoon against the glass bowl extra loud so we could hear what we were missing. We vowed the next night we wouldn't argue. Sometimes it worked.

Toppings were the added bonus. Usually it was nothing fancy, just Hersey's syrup from a can, or better yet Nestles Quick stirred in like a malt. As a grownup I have tried, and made many homemade toppings. These are three of my favorites! Enjoy!

"I doubt whether the world holds for anyone a more soul-stirring surprise than the first adventure with ice cream." ~Heywood Broun

Raspberry Sauce with Grated Dark Chocolate

2 cups (fresh or frozen) raspberries
½ cup sugar
1 teaspoon corn starch
1 dark chocolate candy bar

Place the raspberries and sugar in a sauce pan and heat slowly until the berries burst and become juicy. Then heat to boiling. Reduce heat and add corn starch. (Mix corn starch with water before adding to berries to avoid lumps) Pour over ice cream and grate dark chocolate over the top.

Homemade Hot Fudge and Homemade Caramel are toppings that can be made and placed in half pint size canning jars. These make great gifts with a pretty label and ribbon. You can attach the recipe too unless you want to keep it a "family secret".

Homemade Hot Fudge

8 Tablespoons butter
6 Tablespoons cocoa
1 cup sugar
Dash of salt
1 can evaporated milk
1 teaspoon vanilla

Melt butter in a saucepan. Mix cocoa with sugar and in a separate bowl. Add cocoa sugar mixture to the melted butter. Add can of milk and whisk together. Bring to a boil and simmer for 6 to 7 minutes. Remove from heat. Add Vanilla. Serve over ice cream or pour into three half pint jars to store. Keep refrigerated.

Creamy Caramel Topping

1 cup butter
1 cup white corn syrup
1 can sweetened condensed milk
2 cups brown sugar
⅛ teaspoon salt
1 teaspoon vanilla

In a microwave safe bowl melt butter. Add corn syrup, sugar, milk and salt. Microwave for 15 minutes on High. STIRRING EVERY THREE MINUTES. Remove from microwave and add vanilla. Serve over ice cream or place in half pint jars to store. Keep refrigerated.

** This can be cooked for an additional six minutes in the microwave and poured into a buttered pan to make rich creamy caramels. When cooled, cut into small pieces and wrap in wax paper like a tootsie roll. These are wonderful as a gift in a pretty tin.

The Coldest Spot in the World

Yes, it's true.....I was a Candy Striper. (That's striper with one "p" not two.) For those of you who do not know the difference between a candy striper and a candy stripper let me tell you; one is a non-paid volunteer at a nursing home or hospital and the other is usually well paid, but mostly in ones, fives and tens.

The North Shore Hospital and Nursing Home had a Candy Striper program when I was in 7th and 8th grade. There were five of us from my class who would walk to the hospital after school. There we'd change into the Candy Striper uniform, which was a cute red and white striped jumper with a bib just like overalls. I really liked that dress. We'd all tie our hair up in red ribbons and get to work. Other than babysitting, this was my first "job". I learned a lot. First we had to be on time. We learned to hustle. We had to walk to the hospital from the school, change and punch a timecard by 3:30. Our jobs at the nursing home were not hard work and most of the time it was fun. They had us work in teams of two. We played cards, painted fingernails and read letters to the residents with poor eyesight. Some ladies liked it if we'd do their hair. We'd hear story after story. Sometimes it was the same stories every week but it was fun to hear about their families and their childhoods.

Like me, most started out without running water in their houses. There was a favorite joke by one man, and he would tell over and over. Do you know the coldest spot in the world? *An outhouse seat in January!* This would get us laughing. He didn't like it if you said the punch line though....it was his joke to tell. Between you and me an outhouse seat IS the coldest spot in the world. If you doubt it, plant your bare tushie in a snow bank and give me a call.

I remember that afternoon snack time included juice and the residents could pick the kind of juice they liked. We'd set up little cups with orange juice, apple juice and prune juice. I had never in my life tried prune juice but I loved it. If we had extra cups the nurses would let us each have one cup. I always picked prune juice. I didn't know the effects of prune juice I only knew I liked the flavor, the thickness and the color. To this day I keep individually wrapped prunes in the cupboard for a snack. I laughed as I read a Bundt cake recipe, it called for sweet dried plums…..hmmmm….isn't that a prune? I think they are trying to disguise the truth so those with prune prejudice will get of their high horses and try something new. So a prune juice toast to Candy Stripers everywhere! Enjoy!

Chocolate Prune Bundt Cake

½ cup chopped hazelnuts or walnuts
1 ½ cups flour
1 cup sugar
¾ cup cocoa powder
⅓ cup ground flax seeds
1 ½ teaspoon baking soda
1 ½ teaspoons baking powder
1 teaspoon salt
1 ¼ cups buttermilk
1 cup packed light brown sugar
2 eggs, slightly beaten
¼ cup oil
1 teaspoon vanilla
½ cup hot water
1 cup prune puree (see below)
½ cup semi-sweet chocolate chips
Powdered sugar for dusting

Preheat oven to 350 degrees. Spray Bundt pan well with cooking spray or grease and flour it. Spread nuts on small baking sheet and toast in oven for 5 to 7 minutes. Transfer to plate to cool. Whisk ingredients from flour down to salt in large mixing bowl. Add buttermilk down to vanilla; beat with electric mixer until smooth. Mix hot water and prune puree, then add to batter mixture and stir until well mixed. Fold in chocolate chips and nuts with rubber spatula. Scrape batter into prepared Bundt pan, spreading evenly.

Bake the cake until top springs back when touched lightly and when toothpick comes out clean, 45 to 55 minutes. Cool in pan on wire rack for 10 minutes, and then invert cake onto serving platter or wire rack and dust with powdered sugar. Serve with whipped cream or ice cream if desired.

Notes:
To make prune puree: Place 1 cup of pitted prunes along with 6 Tablespoons hot water into food processor and process until smooth.

Grandma Marion's Oatmeal Prune Bars

1 cup chopped prunes
¼ cup sugar
1 teaspoon grated fresh lemon rind
1 Tablespoon lemon juice
1 ½ cups rolled oats, not quick oats
½ cup brown sugar
¾ cup flour
¼ teaspoon salt
⅔ cup butter

Combine the prunes, sugar, lemon rind and lemon juice in a small pan. Cook, stirring over low heat until thick. Cool completely. In a bowl blend remaining ingredients until crumbly. Pack half the oat mixture firmly into the bottom of a greased 8 inch square pan. Spread with prunes and then top with remaining oat mixture. Pat lightly into the pan. Bake at 350 degrees for 35 minutes.

Pork Medallions with Prunes

½ pound extra-large pitted prunes
1 ½ cups dry white wine
6 pork medallions (about 1 ½ pounds)
Flour for dredging
1 Tablespoon butter
1 Tablespoon vegetable oil
1 Tablespoon red currant jelly
1 teaspoon Dijon mustard
Pinch thyme
Coarse salt and freshly ground pepper to taste
Lemon juice to taste

Simmer the prunes in one cup white wine until tender (about 30 minutes), adding a little water if necessary. Set aside. Wipe the pork medallions dry with paper towels and dredge them lightly with flour. Heat the butter and oil in a large skillet and brown the pork on both sides. Add the remaining wine, red currant jelly, mustard, thyme, salt and pepper. Bring to boil and add the prunes. Cook the medallions, stirring frequently, for four to five minutes or until they have lost their pinkness in the middle. Do not overcook them or they will be tough. If the sauce needs it, add a little lemon juice to cut any sweetness. 4 servings

Oh the Comfort of Jello

I thought I was safe. I curled up in a cozy chair to pull together a few Jello recipes reminiscent of my childhood days and my first cooking experiences. (No microwaves to boil water back then, I had to use a real pan on a gas burner. It felt so grown up.) But just as I was getting comfortable in my recipe hunt, IT jumped out at me, Zucchini Jello Salad. (Yuck!)

I know there are many of you reading this article with gardens overflowing with this, this, well I'm not sure if it's a squash or a vegetable, but I do know I don't like it and I don't want any, thank you very much. My neighbor, who will remain nameless to protect her sweetness, is forever trying to pass me a grocery bag full of zucchini and a recipe card smiling deceptively all the while telling me I can "just grate the zucchini and hide it in the best brownies ever made."… Let me tell you I have made plenty of brownies in my day and they tasted just fine <u>without zucchini</u>. P.S. Zucchini Lovers, if you want the recipe for Zucchini Jello Salad, you'll have to look it up for yourself because I refuse to encourage or support the growing of this, this well, is it a squash or a vegetable??

Back to Jello. This first recipe brought my mother to cult status in Cook County on Halloween night and has kept her there for more than 25 years. She has made Orange Jello Popcorn Balls for her trick or treaters for so long, she now has the children of former trick or treaters at the door on Halloween night. She has confessed she is afraid to stop; they may egg the house in retaliation. While I was living in Minneapolis, Mom suggested that I make Popcorn Balls for my trick or treaters. I gently explained I didn't want to end up on the nightly news.…let's just say homemade treats don't go over so well outside the Cook County line.

*"Raising teenagers is like nailing **Jell-O** to a tree"* ~ *Unknown*

Jello Popcorn Balls – My Mom, LaVonne Anderson

1 cup light corn syrup
½ cup sugar
1 (3 ounce) pkg. any flavor Jello
10 cups unsalted popped popcorn

Mix the corn syrup and the sugar together in a saucepan. Bring this to a boil and remove from heat. Add Jello and stir until dissolved. Pour over large bowl of popped corn. With slightly moistened hands gently form into balls. Place on wax paper to harden. Place in individual baggies to store. Makes 36 Popcorn Balls.

Orange for Halloween, Green and Red for Christmas, Red and Blue for 4th of July......be creative. All flavors are tasty.

Jello Strawberry Bread

3 cups flour
2 cups sugar
1 teaspoon baking soda
1 ½ teaspoon cinnamon
1 (3 ounce) package strawberry Jello
4 eggs – beaten
1 (16 ounce) package frozen strawberries – thawed
1 ¼ cups butter – softened
1 ¼ cups walnuts

Mix dry ingredients, including Jello in a large bowl. Make a well in the center. Mix all remaining ingredients together in a separate bowl, and then pour into the well. Mix well and pour into two greased and floured cake pans. Bake at 350 degrees for one hour.

(This will also make five 3 x 5 gift size loaves. Test for doneness with a toothpick.)

Jello Freezies – Kids Choice

1 (3 ounce) package Jello – any flavor
½ cup sugar
2 cups boiling water
2 cups cold water

Dissolve Jello and sugar in boiling water. Add cold water and pour mixture into 28 small paper cups set on a cookie sheet. Freeze about two hours until almost firm. Insert wooden spoons or sticks and continue to freeze 8 hours or overnight. Peel paper to eat. Easy to make and delicious!

Yes Dear, We have a Deer!

Photo of Gary and Sandy (Holthaus) Anderson taken in their Grandpa and Grandma Allard's yard in the Summer of 1966

When I was growing up in Schroeder, we had a baby deer. Not the kind of deer you keep in a pen or a cage but the kind of baby deer that decided he wanted to be our pet. He came and went as he pleased. He would run through the yard to greet my brother and I when we went outside to play. My parents believe that his mother must have been killed because there was never any sign of her. We named him "Bambi" of course, even though we had never seen the movie. The closest movie theater to us was in Two Harbors and that was over an hour away. I can count on both hands the total number of movies I saw as a child. To the dismay of my sweetest neighbor I have never seen the Disney version of

Bambi. I tell her I had the real thing, why would I want to see a cartoon?? FYI sweet neighbor; Real baby deer don't talk.

Now to be fully honest with you Bambi was probably not drawn to my brother and me as much as he was attracted to my Grandma's apple orchard. She had lots and lots of apple trees. We would try to count them all but we always got confused and argued as to which trees we had counted and which trees we had not. There were so many different kinds we had taste tests and then used the bitten apples apple bombs on our young aunts and uncle when they got off the school bus. It wasn't until later when we learned of the game apple smear (this is where you throw rotten apples in the air and hit them with a tennis racket) that things really got interesting.

To this very day I love the smell of apples baking or cooking. Here are three of my favorite apple recipes. Some have now been modified to utilize modern conveniences like freezer bags and crock pots. I hope you enjoy!

"Any fool can count the seeds in one apple but only God can count the apples from one seed" Robert H. Schuller

Apple Squares

These bars are made in a rimmed baking sheet or a cookie sheet with sides. The crust is on both the top and the bottom. Because the pan is so large I roll the dough out in two sections for the bottom and two sections for the top. It does not have to be perfect as these bars are "rustic" in appearance.

Crust:
3 ½ cups flour
1 cup oil
½ cup water
1 teaspoon salt
1 ½ cup Rice Krispies

Blend ingredients well and divide into two sections. Roll out bottom crust and press into pan. Add one and a half cups Rice Krispies over the crust.

Apple Mix:
10 cups apples
1 cup sugar
1 teaspoon cinnamon
2 Tablespoons butter

Top with baking apples that have been cored and cut up, peeling is optional. Sprinkle with sugar and ground cinnamon. Dot with butter, cut into small pieces. Top with second crust. Bake at 350 degrees for 50 to 60 minutes. When cooled slightly, glaze bars.

Glaze:
1 cup powdered sugar
2 Tablespoons milk or cream
1 Tablespoon softened butter
½ teaspoon vanilla

Mix well and drizzle over bars.

Apple Sauce in the Crock Pot

6 to 8 cooking apples, peeled, cored and cut up
1 cup sugar
1 teaspoon cinnamon
1 ½ teaspoon vanilla or almond extract
¼ teaspoon nutmeg
1 cup of water

Combine all ingredients in your slow cooker. Cook on low five to six hours. Mash to the consistency you like, either smooth or chunky. If you like it really smooth use a sieve. This will keep in the refrigerator for about two weeks or it can be frozen.

Year Round Apple Pie

7 tart apples cored and cut up in slices – (peeling is optional. I like to use Granny Smith apples but use whatever baking apple you have or mix a few different kinds of apples. It just makes the taste more interesting)
1 cup packed brown sugar
2 Tablespoons white sugar
3 Tablespoons flour
½ teaspoon of cinnamon

Place all the ingredients in a one gallon freezer bag. When you want a pie, make a two crust recipe of pie crust and roll out a bottom crust, add slightly thawed apple mix, dot with butter, cover with second crust and cut pie slits. Bake at 400 degrees for 10 minutes then reduce temperature to 375 degrees for 40 to 45 minutes. This is much easier than making and freezing a whole pie.

Ever wanted to be in Three Places at One Time? Visit Schroeder, MN

This is a joint survey commission marker in Schroeder, MN on the shore of Lake Superior where you can actually stand and be in three STATES at one time. This designates where Michigan, Wisconsin and Minnesota all meet.

My friend Colleen and I would play near the survey marker on warm summer days and fantasize about travels to all the great places of the world. Then we would go back to her house and prowl around. Colleen's house was "the best house on earth" because it wasn't <u>just</u> a house it was also the local post office, the laundromat and the grocery store. Her family lived upstairs in what used to be a boarding house. <u>It was also haunted</u>. (This is documented and true; you can look it up in Ghost Stories of the North Shore.) We loved trying to prove to her parents that they had hidden rooms upstairs by measuring and drawing blueprints. Her father would laugh and point out our inadequacies as architects. Still we knew we were on to something. The bodies had to be hidden somewhere!

There was a great claw-footed bath tub that was huge. Colleen and I would fill the tub with pillows and blankets to create our favorite reading spot. She was the one who introduced me to Stephen King novels, which considering the haunted house where we were playing made his stories all the scarier. Her mom would then point out that Colleen had to live and sleep here so we shouldn't try to scare each other so much.

The fact that the survey marker gave us the possibility to be several places at one time just added to the mystique of this place. Today it is no longer a home, it is now the Cross River Heritage Center. Stop by on your way up the shore and ask to see the handprint on the wall that the ghost left behind.

The recipes below are my favorite crock pot meals. By using your crock pot you can free up your time to read a great novel and explore your surroundings. Possibly your home has a hidden room or two???

> *"Nothing in life is to be feared, it is only to*
> *be understood." Marie Curie*

Ground Beef Stroganoff

2 pounds ground beef
2 medium onions, chopped
2 cloves garlic, minced
½ pound fresh mushrooms, sliced
2 teaspoons salt
¼ teaspoon pepper
1 Tablespoon Worcestershire sauce

3 Tablespoons tomato paste
1 cup beef broth

1 cup sour cream
Egg Noodles, prepared

Brown onions and hamburger in skillet. Drain fat. Place all ingredients in the slow cooker except the sour cream and noodles. Cook on low 6 to 8 hours. Just before serving add the sour cream and serve over prepared egg noodles.

Chicken Tetrazzini – from Theresa Heimkes

3 cups cooked chicken (or turkey), diced
½ onion, chopped
1 can cream of chicken soup
¼ cup butter
1 teaspoon garlic powder
1 cup sour cream

8 ounces of thin spaghetti noodles, cooked
2 chicken bouillon cubes
Grated parmesan cheese

Break and cook spaghetti with 2 bouillon cubes in water. Drain but do not rinse. Combine all ingredients and place in buttered 9 x 13 pan. Sprinkle cheese on top. Bake at 325 degrees covered for 15 minutes and uncovered for an additional 30 minutes. Serves 8 to 10.

Sandy Holthaus

Navy Bean Soup

2 cups navy beans
1 cup chopped onion
3 sprigs celery leaves
1 pound ham
1 bay leaf
1 teaspoon salt
6 whole peppercorns

Soak beans in water overnight. Drain and rinse the beans. Combine all ingredients in the slow cooker. Add water to cover. Cook on high 5 to 6 hours. Remove ham and cut into bite size pieces and return these to the pot.

It's a Wonder We Survived
It – Childhood

I had a very active and some might say "dangerous" childhood. To those who shared a childhood like mine (and I know many of you are out there) I know we shake our heads in wonderment as we buckle, strap and helmet our children through their days.

I am not just talking about my dad smoking in the car and the house (second hand smoke) which he did, I'm referring to the rough and tumble games we would not even consider letting our kids partake in today.

Ages 0 to 3 - Catch the baby (Shaken Baby Syndrome) was a favorite in our house. My dad and one of his friends would stand a distance apart and throw my brother and me laughing and screaming through the air across the living room. My mom would hide her eyes and visibly pray throughout the game. We loved it! We were never dropped on our heads that I remember – but then again maybe I wouldn't remember – or would I?

Ages 3 to 6 - We would slide at great speeds on the rail sled down Grandma's driveway (no helmets or mouth guards). Do those rail sleds REALLY TURN? Well mine didn't and I hit my Great Aunt Vivian's black car head on. (Closed head injury?) My baby teeth turned black but they tightened right back up and were fine in a couple of days.

Ages 7 to 9 - Tramping through the woods building forts and (shhhhh) fires.

Ages 10 to 15 - In the Summers we would ride our 10 speed bikes (What's a bike helmet?) down the Cramer Road to the Temperance River and swim (No life jackets, kick boards or water wings) in the canyons. Back then there was a rope that hung down so the locals could climb up and swim in the falls (Drowning). The real daring people, like my brother Gary, would jump from the cliffs into the freezing cold water (Hypothermia). The tourists (Stranger danger) would shake their heads in disbelief. These same tourists would often ask us for directions and we would fake foreign accents and send them the wrong way just for fun. My best friend Jenny could do a great Norwegian spiel.

But at the end of every day what I remember the most is coming home to a "sit down" dinner with the whole family and talking about our day. We KNEW Mom and Dad would always be there if we ever got in to any REAL trouble. I guess not all child protection devices are visible; love and security might be the best "safety net" of all.

Take some chances, live dangerously and try some of these "risky" dinners in your house this week.

> *"If no one ever took risks, Michelangelo would have painted on the Sistine floor." – Neil Simon*

Orange Thyme Crock Pot Chicken

6 ounce can frozen orange juice
½ teaspoon thyme
Dash ground nutmeg
Dash garlic powder
6 boneless skinless chicken breast halves
¼ cup water
2 Tablespoons cornstarch

Combine thawed orange juice concentrate (not regular orange juice) in a bowl with the spices. Dip each piece of chicken into the orange mixture and coat completely. Place in crock pot. Pour the leftover mixture over the chicken. Cover and cook on low for 6 to 7 hours on high for 4 hours. When chicken is done, remove and keep warm, pour juice from crock pot into a saucepan. Mix corn starch with water and stir into pan with juice. Cook over medium heat, stirring constantly, until thick and bubbly. Serve over the chicken. This is great served with brown rice.

Cube Steaks with Blue Cheese

6 cube steaks
Salt and pepper to taste
6 Tablespoons crumbled blue cheese
¼ cup red onion, finely chopped

Preheat broiler. Meanwhile, in a skillet, brown cube steak to your liking, salt and pepper to taste. Place beef on broiler pan and top each steak with cheese and onion. Place under broiler to melt and serve. These steaks are delicious served with baked potatoes.

Apricot Fish

½ cup apricot preserves
2 Tablespoons white vinegar
½ teaspoon tarragon
6 fish fillets (I like a white fish)

Preheat broiler. In a small bowl, mix preserves, vinegar and tarragon. Place fish on broiler pan and broil about 4 minutes on each side. One minute before fish is ready brush with preserve mixture and broil an additional minute.

The Wreath, the Real
Nature of Love

We see wreaths everywhere at Christmas time and to most people they are lush and green and represent a simple sign of the season. To me a wreath represents so much more, hours of hard work, delayed gratification and best of all, money of my own. Yes we made wreaths! The Anderson Family of Schroeder has been making Christmas wreaths for as long as I can remember. The process would start long before winter though. In the Fall my mom would take my brother and me out to the woods and set a laundry basket between us to pick princess pine. Lots of princess pine! This is a short ground covering that truly resembles a miniature tree. We would pull it up leaves, grass and all just to fill the basket faster but we soon learned there was a price to pay for shortcuts! Pine cleaning time! I remember standing by the trash can in my footie jammies when I was about four years old begging my parents to let me go to bed so I wouldn't have to clean the pine!

Next came the cutting of fresh cedar boughs to mix with the princess pine. All the boughs have to be snipped into small florets to add to the pine bunches. When both the pine and cedar where ready, we sat at a card table nightly and made wreathes. Dozens and dozens of wreaths. My brother and I would make the bunches, my dad would wrap them around old wire coat hangers that he had pulled to be round. Dad whistled the whole time, except when he was knocking on the table for us to hurry it up. My mom was the wreath decorator. She used handmade red bows and pine cones. Back then she sometimes used silver spray paint to give the wreath an extra glow but now the more natural look is in.

After the wreathes were made, then came sales! My mom is a natural born meticulous record keeper. She could tell you today anyone who bought a wreath for the last 40 years. She would give my brother and me the list of customers who bought wreaths the previous year and we would have to pull a chair up to the rotary phone and make sales calls. (Not an easy feat on a seven party house line. If you don't know what a party line is, call me, you won't believe it.) This taught me not to be intimidated by the phone and talking to people I don't know. The rest of the wreaths were loaded into the back seat of the car and we went selling door to door. Who wouldn't buy a wreath from a freezing child with a red nose??? "$2.50 please."

The real payoff came at the end of the season. Mom and Dad would sit down and show us the numbers, (profits after expenses divided by four.) We would then take our hard earned money to the Grand Marais Ben Franklin and do our secret Christmas shopping. If you've ever been to the Grand Marais Ben Franklin you know you can buy ANYTHING and EVERYTHING there!

The tradition of the Anderson wreaths continues to this day with neighbor kids learning the same valuable lessons we learned: hard work, no short cuts, look people in the eye, say thank you, shake hands, introduce yourself on the phone because they can't see you, profit always comes after expenses, and spend your money wisely because it's easier spent than made. Amen! Merry Christmas to you all!

> *"The wreath symbolizes the real nature of love. Real love never ceases. Love is one continuous round of affection"* ~ *From the True Meaning of Christmas*

Chocolate Popovers

1 cup flour
¼ cup sugar
2 Tablespoons cocoa
¼ teaspoon salt
4 eggs
1 cup milk
2 Tablespoons butter, melted
½ teaspoon vanilla
Powdered sugar

Position oven rack to the lower third of the oven. Preheat to 375 degrees. Grease six cup popover pan or six custard cups. If using custard cups set them on a rimmed baking sheet for easier transfers. Mix all dry ingredients; set aside. Beat eggs in a large bowl with an electric mixer for one minute on low speed. Beat in milk, butter and vanilla. Slowly beat in flour mixture until smooth. Pour batter into prepared pans. Bake 50 minutes. Immediately remove popovers to wire rack and generously sprinkle with powdered sugar.

Cherry Eggnog Quick Bread

2 ½ half cups flour
¾ cup sugar
1 Tablespoon baking powder
½ teaspoon nutmeg
1 ¼ cup dairy eggnog
6 Tablespoons butter, melted
2 eggs, slightly beaten
½ cup chopped pecans
½ cup chopped candied red cherries

Preheat oven to 350 degrees. Grease three mini loaf pans. Mix dry ingredients in a large bowl. Stir in eggnog, melted butter, eggs and vanilla together in a separate bowl. Slowly add eggnog mixture to flour mixture. Mix just until all ingredients are well moistened. Fold in pecans and cherries. Spoon into prepared pans. Bake 35 to 40 minutes. Test with toothpick. Cool in pans 15 minutes and remove to finish cooling on a wire rack.

Kahlua Hot Spiced Apple Cider

1 ½ ounces Kahlua
1 cup hot apple cider
1 cinnamon stick

Pour Kahlua into mug and carefully add the hot cider. Stir with a cinnamon stick. Makes one serving. This is my favorite hot drink for the holidays!

Playing Chicken!

When I was about five or so I wanted a playhouse more than anything. Not the "little tyke" plastic kind of playhouse but a small wooden house with a door and a window where I could pretend to do all the things I do today, only now, it's my job. I think for most of us cleaning, cooking and vacuuming had much more appeal at the age of five.

We had a small broken down old tool shed that I kind of converted into my play home but then my dad convinced me to give it up with the promise that he would later build me a log playhouse complete with a door and everything. What would Dad want with an old tool shed you ask? I was curious also but then "they" came; in the mail no less. Chirping and pecking – baby chicks! They were so cute, all yellow and downy…we kept them inside our house for a little while until they were old enough to move into the tool shed/ playhouse/chicken coop. There were about 50 of them. They would scratch and dig at the ground for whatever they could find. It was fun to watch them strut around like big chickens which they soon became. These were fast growing meat chickens. I guess some of you know what comes next for "meat chickens". GULP! Butchering time. I was horrified as Mom and Dad chopped the heads off each and every one with a hatchet. But soon it turned into a *"cartoon like"* experience because chickens don't know that they have lost their heads right away. They actually can run quite far without it. My brother and I had the job to follow them and pick them up when they stopped running so we wouldn't lose any under an old car or something. I know this sounds macabre at its best, but to a four and five year old it was kind of like chasing road runner and it soon turned into a game. To this day I really like chicken and I eat it all the time so I guess the experience didn't scar me for life.

As for the log playhouse...we got as far as the floor then my dad hacked his leg with the draw knife while trying to peel poplar logs for the walls - that ended that. After a few butterfly band-aids he healed right up but you can still feel the dent in his leg bone to this day. I played on that platform for years and just pretended I had walls and a door. Seriously, I would only let other kids come onto the platform threw the door that was drawn out onto the wood floor. (You work with what you have my friends.)

Not a lot of people make homemade chicken noodle soup anymore because it takes a whole day and it's kind of putsy. I love it! And I like to make it from scratch not just because it tastes better but it is a whole household experience. What I mean is the entire house smells like soup! When the kids and Mike come home they inhale deeply and that gets their stomachs rumbling. I really like to make it for weekend guests because we nibble at it on Saturday and Sunday whenever anyone needs a little snack.

I hope you take the time to try this recipe. You can skip the homemade noodle part if that is just "over the top" for you. Store bought noodles, either dried or from the freezer case works just as well. Don't skip the whole cut up chicken though; using frozen, boneless, skinless chicken breast doesn't give the soup the same flavor or your home the same wonderful smell.

Homemade Chicken Noodle Soup

Fill a large stock pot with cold water. (Don't use hot water as it seals in the chicken flavor too fast and you don't get the best broth.) Add one whole, cut up chicken, one large onion chopped, a teaspoon of dried rosemary and chicken bouillon. You can use cubes or crystals. I use about five of the cubes. Let this simmer for several hours until the chicken starts to fall off the bones. While the chicken is cooking I make the noodles.

For the noodles: Place two cups of flour in a mound on the counter, sprinkle with one half a teaspoons of salt then scoop into a pile and make a well. (Kind of like a volcano) Add two beaten eggs and two teaspoons of milk. Knead until dough is soft and elastic, add additional milk if necessary. Cover and let dough rest for ten minutes. Divide dough into four equal parts. Roll out on a lightly floured surface into a 12 inch square into one/sixteenth inch thick. Cut into strips about a half inch wide. I cut the strips with a pizza cutter three to four inches long. Set aside and continue with the rest of the dough. Let the noodles dry until soup is ready.

Meanwhile check the chicken and see if it is pulling from the bones. Use a slotted spoon to take the chicken pieces out of the broth. Set these in a bowl to cool. Raise the heat on the broth to a low boil and add cut up potatoes and carrots. (You can use fresh corn or celery if you like, I don't but my sister-cousin does. This is where we disagree on who makes the best soup!) Cook these until the veggies are tender. (About 20 minutes) While veggies are cooking you can clean the chicken. There is no easy way to do this - you have to use your hands. Pull the skin off the chicken and pull the chicken from the bones. Pick only the meat pieces and discard the rest. I then pull or cut the chicken meat into bite size pieces. Add the meat and the noodles back to the gently simmering broth, cook for two to five minutes until the noodles are tender. At this time the broth may need a little extra seasoning and thickening. Do this to your preference. Sometimes it seems like it takes quite a bit of salt but potatoes really pull a lot of salt from the broth. Serve with fresh bread and real butter! This makes enough soup to share with neighbors too!

> *"As for butter versus margarine, I trust the cows*
> *more than the chemists."* ~ *Joan Gussow*

If You Give A Moose A Muffin.......

Photo taken by Misty Schliep of her son Jory and the moose,
Murphy, who visits them at their cabin on Isle Royle.

If You Give A Moose A Muffin....

This is one of my favorite children's books written by Laura Numeroff. She and the illustrator, Felicia Bond, make this moose seem clever sweet, kind and resourceful (he can even make sock puppets). But in the wild meeting a moose can be a much different story. We lived on forty acres that backed up to county land and a power line. Wild life of all kinds roamed these woods and sometimes into our yard. This included bear, bobcats, deer and every so often a moose or two. My dad always said the moose was probably the most dangerous. This was verified by our neighbor who sat in a tree for several hours waiting for a Bull Moose to let him down. (We teased him that the Bull Moose must have thought he was a girl moose.) One particular day we were playing outside when a mother moose walked right up the road with TWO calves! My mom rushed us inside but we watched her from the windows. The people and houses did not seem to bother her in the least.

When my mother turned sixty we surprised her with a boat trip to Isle Royal for the day. All of us wanted to see a moose in the worst way and we had heard that several were roaming the island that year. The guide said we would need to take a three mile hike to get to where the moose were last sighted. My youngest was only three at the time and I didn't think he was up to walking three miles and I surely wasn't up to carrying him three miles so he and I opted to stay at the landing and play by the water. My mom stayed also to keep us company. No sooner had the hikers left when three VERY LARGE moose came out of the woods to graze in the shallow water on the swamp grass in the bay. Mom, Ben and I took wonderful pictures and watched them as they munch uncaring or unnoticing our excitement. Of course in typical moose fashion they decided to return to the deep woods just as our group of tired hikers returned after their long walk, greatly disappointed that they hadn't see a thing! I tell you moose are a surly bunch!

The above picture, taken near Wisconsin of two albino moose. The chance of seeing an albino moose is astronomical and the chance of seeing two – well buy a lottery ticket my friend – because the odds are almost impossible.

Blueberry Muffins

½ butter
1 ½ cups of sugar
2 eggs
½ cup milk
½ teaspoon salt
2 teaspoons baking powder
2 cups flour

2 ½ cups blueberries (fresh or frozen)

Using a spoon mix all ingredients except the blueberries, (Do not use a mixer on muffins or they will get tough.) Gently fold berries into batter. Line sixteen muffin cups with paper liners. Fill each ¾ full with batter and add a teaspoon of sugar to the top of each one. (I use sugar mixed with cinnamon but that's a personal preference.) Place water in the unused muffin cups so all will bake evenly. Bake at 375 degrees for 25 to 30 minutes.

Banana Muffins (These are a family favorite! We add chocolate chips also!)

2 cups sugar
½ cup shortening
2 Tablespoons oil
2 cups mashed bananas
3 eggs
2 ¼ cups flour
2 ½ teaspoons baking soda
2 ½ teaspoons baking powder
¾ teaspoon salt
¾ teaspoons vanilla
1 ½ teaspoons lemon juice
1 cup buttermilk (I keep powdered buttermilk on hand and mix it up as I need it.)

Cream sugar, shortening and oil. Add bananas and cream well. Add eggs and mix well. Combine all dry ingredients and add to the first mixture. Then add vanilla and lemon juice. Mix well at low speed and gradually add the buttermilk. Mix at medium speed for three minutes. (Here is where you can fold in a cup or so of chocolate chips.) Put into greased or paper lined muffin pans. Makes about two dozen. Bake at 350 degrees for about 20 minutes.

Morning Glory Muffins

1 cup flour
¾ cup sugar
1 teaspoon baking soda
¼ teaspoon salt
1 teaspoon of ground cinnamon
1 cup grated carrots
¼ cup raisins
¼ cup flake coconut
2 eggs
7 Tablespoons oil
1 small apple, chopped
1 teaspoon vanilla

Combine flour, sugar, baking soda, salt and cinnamon. Add carrots, raisins and coconut. Mix well. In a separate bowl mix eggs, oil, apple and vanilla. Add egg mixture to flour mixture. Stir to blend, then spoon into 12 greased muffin cups. Bake at 350 degrees for 15 to 18 minutes. Let rest for five minutes then serve.

Going Bananas!

Who doesn't remember their first paying job? Or their first boss? I remember mine all too well. His name was Bill. He moved to Schroeder when he bought Lamb's Grocery Store. The post office was also in the building across the room but he didn't run that... he thought it took up valuable store space and he told you that every day! (For my thinking it was the only reason most of the locals stopped by.) You see, Bill wasn't a warm and fuzzy kind of guy. He didn't understand small town communication etiquette either. If he had a problem with you he told you, RIGHT TO YOUR FACE. (Everyone knows that if you have a problem with someone in a small town you either told the gas man's wife who had a seven party phone line or the Avon lady. These ladies would make sure you got the message in a subtle, tactful manner over a cup of coffee and fingernail polish.)

I liked Bill because I like characters and he was probably the biggest character we had in the whole Schroeder population of 400. He was a big man with a big laugh and he loved *"getting peoples goat"* as my mom used to say. Teasing the locals was his favorite entertainment.

Bill also serviced the Iron Orr boats that docked in Schroeder for supplies. To him "supplies" included a variety of magazines that came in "brown wrappers" if you know what I'm talking about. The ladies in town had to reach right past these "books" to get at their Ladies Home Journal. Bill would laugh as their hands would shake and they would blush. He also enjoyed walking through the store in nothing but his T-shirt and boxers, as he lived in the house upstairs. He would time it just as I had a line of customers checking out. I would have to fake smile and act like I didn't actually see him skirting through the back of the store.

The towns' people would shake their heads and ask me if the pay was worth it. Some offered me other employment.

Bill taught me a lot. He taught me how to get teased to the point you want to scream but be forced to pretend it didn't bother you. (His nickname for me was Spicy Meatball.) He also, through his twisted value system, taught me to stand up against corporate waste and injustice - all over a case of bananas. Stick with me on this one....I found a spoiled case of bananas in the cooler. Bill told me to throw them away. I said many of the ladies in town would probably like them for baking banana bread and asked if he wanted to give them away. To my shock he said "No, throw them away." I asked why you would rather throw something away than to give it away if it could be used?? He said "Meatball, I SELL food, I don't GIVE it away." So I asked if *I* could give them away. (That way he could keep his reputation as a grouch.) He said "No you can't give them away because you don't own them and you can't give away something that isn't yours." Hmm, OK he had a point there. So I asked "If I owned them, then could I give them away??" He conceded, "Yes, Spicy Meatball if you owned them you could do whatever you wanted with them." Long story short, I bought them. A huge case of rotten bananas!!! At 19 cents a pound! (He wouldn't even cut me a deal) I was fuming as I weighed each and every pound. I sure showed him!! I bought 50 pound of rotting smelling bananas... that he was just going to throw away...Hey, did I pay the man $9.50 for his garbage??? Yeah I sure showed him, he laughed over that for years and never let me forget it!! I was so sad to learn that Bill was killed while skiing at Lutsen Resort. I'm positive he died the way he lived, fast, furious and laughing at the locals! Peace to you Bill! Your Spicy Meatball

> *"No one can drive us crazy unless we give them the keys." Doug Horton*

In my ode to Bill I am giving you my favorite
banana recipes. Use them well...

Aunt Donna's Banana Bread

⅔ cups sugar
⅓ cup shortening
1 ¾ cups flour
2 teaspoons baking powder
½ teaspoon salt
¼ teaspoon soda
2 eggs
1 cup mashed bananas
1 teaspoon vanilla

In a mixing bowl, cream sugar and shortening. Add two eggs and
beat well with bananas and vanilla. Add dry ingredients, mix
well. Place batter into greased loaf pan and bake at 350 degrees
for one hour.

Mom's Banana Crème Pie

You will need:
Homemade Pudding – see below
Bottom Shell Pie Crust – Baked
Sliced Fresh Bananas
Whipped Cream for topping

Homemade Pudding:

⅔ cups sugar
3 Tablespoons corn starch
½ teaspoon salt
3 cups milk
3 egg yolks

1 Tablespoon butter
1 ½ teaspoons vanilla

In a saucepan mix sugar, corn starch, and salt. Gradually stir in milk and heat over medium heat until thickens and boils, boil one minute. Watch and stir constantly! Beat egg yolks into a bowl and gradually add one half of hot mixture to eggs. Once mixed well and add egg mixture back to pan. Heat and boil one additional minute. Remove from heat and stir in butter and vanilla. Cool slightly. Layer over baked pie shell with sliced bananas. Top with whipped cream. Chill and serve.

Apple Banana Fruit Smoothies

1 small banana
1 cup Granny Smith Apple juice – no sugar added
Five ice cubes
Blend well in a blender on high. Makes one serving.

Childhood Lessons 101

I have been thinking a lot about interest calculations lately and how much we really pay for our houses. Do you realize that a mortgage of $150,000.00 at a rate of 6% for 30 years will cost you about $324,000.00? This is $174,000.00 more than the purchase price of your home! I hear you saying, "Yes Sandy; we know that is Interest Calculation 101." (AKA Reality...) But bear with me, when I was young I actually knew people who NEVER had a mortgage payment EVER. And they wouldn't dream of borrowing $150K from any bank or anybody! My parents, young and just starting out, bought 40 acres with a two room cabin. The cabin had electricity but no running water. (My Dad says we ALWAYS had running water...we had to RUN get it and RUN it home!) One room was made into a living room and the other into a kitchen. There was a small shed on the back that was used for two tiny bedrooms that shared one closet. The closet didn't have a back on it so it was fun to climb right on through. Mom and Dad took over small monthly payments and we made do until enough money could be saved to add a bathroom and a larger kitchen. ("Made do" meaning five years and three kids later.) The old kitchen then became the living room, the living room became Mom and Dad's bedroom and my younger brother and I now each had a room of our own. (My older brother had passed away as an infant) We were in kindergarten by then and it was such a treat to have running water! (No more frozen bottoms from the outhouse either!)

It just didn't seem odd to me then that we lived a certain way that was any different from anyone else. I had friends whose parents built basements and the whole family lived in the basement for years until they could afford to build the actual house on top of the foundation. The community seemed to build as the money came in – no money – no building. Back to interest calculations: I am awed to think how much money my parents and neighbors actually SAVED by this "debt free" way of thinking. Thousands of dollars!

My parents added on again when my brother and I were in about fifth grade. We tore off the old shed off the back of the house and built a partial basement, two bedrooms and an upstairs. How many kids can say they pounded the nails that built their bedroom floor? We even got to pick out our bedroom paneling and closet doors. No more crawling through the back of the closet which by this time had become more irritating than entertaining. My entire room was my favorite color, green – the carpet, the door and even the ceiling! (My parents might not have had money pouring out of their pockets but they were pretty easy going.)

Saving money meant really saving. I never saw a credit card used in our household until after I graduated from high school. Only then it was because it made ordering easier from stores and catalogs. Before that time my mother would wait until we had enough money in the checkbook to get the Sears and Roebuck school clothes we wanted. I remember arguing with my mom once that she MUST have money because she HAD CHECKS! (That lead to lesson two – Checkbook 101.)

The absolute greatest gift I was ever given as a child was a savings book from my Grandma Anderson. She started one out for each of us as babies by putting $5.00 in it. Every time we had money we would take it to the bank and the teller would write it in our little books and give us a sucker. As we grew into our teens we probably had more withdrawals than deposits but you could see the balance go up and down and understand the history of where your money went with a quick glance through the book. (Lesson three - Savings 101) The bank was in Grand Marais and close to Ben Franklin so it was easy to run over and withdraw just enough for the new John Denver album when it came out. Shopping took serious thought. Not a lot of impulse buying here just that record alone was worth ten hours of babysitting money but John was worth it! I still have this record in my living room ready for a spin on the turntable.

Today I appreciate these lessons more than ever and I wish we lived in a society that encouraged, supported and promoted a debt free way of life – let's make it from scratch and pay as we go!

"Today, there are three kinds of people: the haves, the have-nots, and the have-not-paid-for-what-they-have." ~ Earl Wilson

Favorite German Scratch Recipes

Gewürz Kuchen (SpiceCake)

½ cup shortening
1 cup sugar
¼ teaspoon salt
1 egg
1 cup raisins
½ teaspoon cinnamon
2 cups of flour
1 cup sour milk *
1 teaspoon baking soda

Cream shortening with sugar and salt, add egg and beat well. Blend in raisins and cinnamon. Add flour alternately with sour milk and soda. Blend well. Bake in loaf pan for one hour at 350 degrees. * Sour milk can be made by adding a teaspoon of lemon juice or vinegar to regular milk and let it sit for a minute or two.

Krummen Kuchen (Crumb Cake)

2 cups brown sugar
1 Tablespoon lard (I use real butter)
2 cups flour
½ teaspoon salt

1 cup sour milk *
1 teaspoon soda
2 eggs
1 teaspoon vanilla or almond extract

Mix sugar and lard together. Take out a scant cup of the mixture and set it aside. To the remaining add sour milk in which the soda has been dissolved, flour, salt, eggs and flavoring. Mix well and pour into a greased and floured 9 by 13 cake pan. Spread the scant cup of crumbs over the top and bake at 350 degrees for 25 to 30 minutes. * Sour milk can be made by adding a teaspoon of lemon juice or vinegar to regular milk and let it sit for a minute or two.

Grosse Pfannkuchen (Dessert Pancakes)

I make these with a skillet that has an oven safe handle.

½ cup flour
½ cup milk
½ teaspoon salt
2 eggs
Dash ground nutmeg
4 Tablespoons butter

Stir milk slowly into flour mixed with salt and nutmeg, making a smooth, thin batter. Add eggs one at a time beating well after each addition. Preheat oven to 350 degrees. Place skillet and butter in the oven just until butter is melted. Add mixture and bake 10 to 12 minutes. Pancake will be really puffy but it settles as it cools so serve it right away with butter and syrup or a fruit sauce of your choice. Recipe makes one pfannkuchen.

Grow Your Garden

I love to garden, as does my sister-cousin Dawn, who is as close to me as any sister would be. We have decided that this "green thumb" must skip a generation because our Grandmothers were both wonderful gardeners while our mothers only dabbled in it here and there. Dawn is somewhat older than I am (four years) so she has memories of our childhood that greatly differ from mine so we (as sisters would) tend to gently dispute the accuracy of each other's individual memories. What I do remember is that she had little time for me one particular summer at her family's dairy farm in Rochester. She was 14 and I was ten. She was into boys, hair and makeup; I was into jumping off the hay bales and running around the farm with her younger brother, Steven. She tried to give me beauty tips, pushing back my cuticles and styling my hair but I just rolled my eyes and ran away to practice shooting BB guns with the boys. Her attention to beauty must have paid off as this was the summer she met the boyfriend of all boyfriends whom she has now been dating / married to for almost 40 years. Who knew clean cuticles could attract a long lasting suitor??

My job on the farm that year was to wash the cow teats so that my uncle could hook them up to the milking machine. Day one I was kicked by no less than three cows. My uncle Norman couldn't believe it until he felt the "icy cold" water I was using! I guess the lady cows like warm washcloths just like we do.

My maternal grandparents lived on a farm in Byron, MN which wasn't too far from Rochester. This is the farm that my mother grew up on until she was in tenth grade when her family moved to the North Shore. (It is well know that my Grandpa Haven couldn't stay anywhere for more than ten years. So he moved my grandma around a lot.) My Grandma Isabelle's garden in Byron was like the secret garden because it was surrounded by huge trees and only had a small path leading to it from the yard. There was a gully on one side that grandma would tell the grandkids to throw the rotten tomatoes into; and before we knew it there were tomato plants everywhere! These we could use for tomato wars or target practice.

Her mother, my Great Grandma Moulton, lived right in Rochester and she had a back yard garden that was mostly flowers and berries. I loved going to her house because she had two screen porches side by side and you could pretend you had your own little house with a neighbor next door. She had the most beautiful African Violets that bloomed in her bedroom window year around. She kept them on a stair step kind of plant holder that made them look like they were a cascade of pink and purple flowers. She would teach me how to pick off the dead flowers so more flowers would come. I think sometimes about trying my hand at violets just to see if I inherited the gift, I just need to find a stair step plant holder.

Both grandmothers canned everything. What I remember most would be the pickles. From dill pickles, to watermelon rind, to these really sweet pickles that had so much green food coloring in them they looked like they were made of plastic. Jars and jars of canned goods would be lined up in the dirt cellar at the farm in Byron. Grandma would send us down there but I would always skedaddle as that was not my favorite place to go! Dark and spidery!

If you get the chance this summer, try your hand at homemade pickles. I promise you they are not hard and if you don't want to grow the cucumbers yourself you can get a whole pail at the Flea Market that is ready to go. Watermelon rinds are even easier to come by around the fourth of July! Just follow the bees!

"Show me your garden and shall tell you what you are." Alfred Austin

Ice Box Hamburger Pickles

These are sweet pickles not dill like store bought hamburger pickles. This is an easy recipe for older children to make and its good practice to learn slicing with a knife or a mandolin.

6 cups unpeeled cucumbers, sliced thin
1 cup onions, sliced thin
1 green pepper, seeded and sliced thin (optional)
1 cup vinegar
2 cups sugar
1 Tablespoon salt

Mix all ingredients. Stir well and place in glass jars. These will keep for weeks in the ice box. Let sit for about a week before eating.

Grandma's 11 Day Sweet Pickles

For this recipe you need a two gallon jar and eleven days, so don't make these if you're on your way out of town.

Fill a two gallon jar with sliced cucumbers. (I slice them thicker, about a half an inch and I use the medium sized cucumbers.) Add two teaspoons of alum and one teaspoon salt to the jar. Fill with boiling water. Do this every day for seven days in a row. Throw the old brine away and make new each day. On the 8th day drain brine, throw it away and make a syrup with six cups of sugar, two quarts of vinegar, one quart water, a 3 ounce box of pickling spices wrapped in cheesecloth, and 5 ounces of green food coloring. Heat until sugar is dissolved and pour over pickles. On the 9th day pour the syrup into a pan and add three more cups of sugar, additional green food coloring and reheat. Pour over pickles. On the 10th day pour syrup into a pan and add three more cups of sugar and even more green food coloring. Reheat and pour over pickles. On the eleventh day put pickles into jars and seal. The very best pickles you ever ate!

Watermelon Rind Pickles

Pickles:

12 cups watermelon rind (outer green peeled, pink pulp removed, use just the white part)
Enough Cold water to cover
1 Tablespoon powdered alum

Syrup:

8 cups sugar
4 cups water
4 cups vinegar
2 Tablespoons whole allspice
2 Tablespoons whole cloves
10 cinnamon sticks

Remove all pink pulp from rind and peel. Cut in one inch cubes. Combine cold water and alum; pour over rind. Let stand 1 hour. Drain. Cover with fresh cold water. Simmer 1 hour or until tender. Drain. Tie spices in a cheesecloth. Combine vinegar, water and sugar. Heat until sugar dissolves. Add spice bag and rind. Simmer gently 2 hours. Pack rind in hot sterile jars. Fill with boiling hot syrup. Seal. Yield: approx. 12 half pints.

Ever Smelled a Smelt?

When I read that South Haven was hosting a smelt fry this really brought back some memories for me. As a child the smelt would run on the Cross River right in Schroeder. (My dad teased us "How could fish run??" Think about it.) Running smelt always seemed to be late at night when it was really, really dark. We all know that country dark is different than city dark. You truly cannot see your own hand in front of your face. We would work our way down to the mouth of the river using big flashlights and balancing long handle fishing nets. My brother and I loved it. The whole town would be down by the water. One lady told me that you had to bite the head off your first smelt of the season to ensure a good run next year. I thought she was joking, trust me, she wasn't. I guess she was celebrating the good fishing with a good beer. One year I thought I should try to save every smelt that had washed up on the beach by throwing them back in the water and setting them "free". My version of saving a beached whale. The beach bar hoppers thought this was pretty funny.

We would then take our haul home and even though I know you won't believe this I swear to the Holy Heavens that it is true, my dad would *filet* the smelt. These tiny itty bitty filets were no bigger than extra small potato chips! (Think about minnow filets...) My mom would then deep fry them in beer batter and we would gobble them up before they even had a chance to cool on the paper towels. Crispy and delicious!

People of course tried to be creative in their use of smelt, being they were free and plentiful in those days, but success was not in their favor. One man attempted to feed his sled dogs a diet of smelt but there wasn't enough nutritional value to keep the dogs healthy. The dogs had no energy to pull his dog sled.

My grandmother though was probably the most creative and from the onset it seemed she had a good idea. She had heard that fish emulsion was a good fertilizer for gardens. Like most ideas this grew to a point of excitement as she pictured having the most wonderful vegetable garden around. She tilled the smelt into the soil and carefully planted her seedlings and seeds. The garden looked beautiful. Grandma failed to think of one other sea creature of the North Shore ....Seagulls! Let me tell you those birds can smell a fish for miles and when they flock, they flock. They also called all their friends to join the buffet. They made short work of her garden. Tearing up all its plants and seeds, paying no mind to the small screaming woman with a broom! Trust me it wasn't funny that day but whenever I see a seagull I think of Grandma. Those birds could smell a smelt!

> *"Everybody is a genius. But if you judge a fish by its ability to climb a tree, it will live its whole life believing that it is stupid."* ~ *Albert Einstein*

I don't have access to the smelt like I use to but here are a few fishy recipes to try!

Honey Fried Walleye Fillets

6 large walleye fillets
⅔ cup oil
1egg, beaten
1 Tablespoon honey
1 ½ cup crushed soda crackers
½ cup flour
½ teaspoon salt
½ teaspoon pepper

Dry fillets on paper towel. Heat oil in skillet. Combine eggs and honey in one bowl. Mix dry ingredients in a separate shallow bowl. Dip fillets into the egg mixture then press firmly into the dry mixture. Fry about three minutes on each side in the preheated oil.

Tasty Tartar Sauce – by Joy Carlson

2 cups real mayonnaise
1 Tablespoon lemon juice
⅓ cup red onion – chopped fine
1 large dill pickle – chopped fine
1 Tablespoon capers
1 teaspoon parsley
1 teaspoon dill weed
½ teaspoon Accent

Mix well. Store refrigerated.

Fish Cakes

It seems everyone has a favorite fishcake recipe. I like this one because I don't have a meat grinder and I can use the blender.

¾ cup milk
1 egg
1 Tablespoon oil
1 teaspoon cornstarch
½ small onion
¼ teaspoon mace
Dash of pepper
2 cups herring or northern fillets cut into 1 inch pieces
1 teaspoon salt

In the blender combine milk, egg, oil, cornstarch, onion mace and pepper. Add fish slowly with short spurts. (Over blending will make the mixture too soupy...use caution. If mixture is too thick add a small amount of milk.) Pour mixture into a bowl and add salt. Cover the bottom of a skillet with oil and heat. Drop fish into pan with a teaspoon or a small ice cream scoop. Fry until golden on both sides.

Big Dreams

I guess you could say I am an idea person. It seems my brain is always spinning new yarns. This has been a part of my make-up for as long as I can remember and I guess I was so very lucky to grow up with parents that supported each new idea with the same enthusiasm I had. They would listen as I explained how I wanted to decorate my first house with old steering wheels from classic cars and then spend hours trekking through junk yards trying to find just the right wheel. Or when I had the idea I had to make tiny bird houses from drift wood…before I knew it Dad had the boat loaded and we were cruising along the shore of Dyers Lake gathering weathered wood. There were no "nay sayers" in our house, no rolling eyes and here she goes again. I never heard the term "hair brained idea" until I was married! (and that came from Mike.) I was thinking of all of this because I grew up with so many people who had big dreams, and my class reunion was just around the corner.

As timing would have it, I was cleaning out my garage with my GPO (gorgeous personal organizer) and we came across a box of high school papers. I didn't take the time to sort through it then but the other day I sat down and found some very interesting readings. I had two really great friends when I was in ninth grade. LeAnn Freeberg and Terry Backlund. I found old notes and letters LeAnn and I would send back and forth. LeAnn was a dreamer who saw herself as a successful business owner one day. She knew what she wanted and started going to trade school during the summer. By the time we graduated she had her cosmetology licensed and she owned her own beauty shop by our 5th year class reunion. Now she owns 1010 Design an award winning Interior

Design Company. (10/10 is my birthday so I tease her that she named her store after me.)

In my stash of papers I also found Terry Backlund's drivers permit. (You think you don't know who Terry Backlund is but my guess is if you've been to Grand Marais you probably do.) Why I would have his permit, I don't remember but he either gave it to me or I stole it knowing he would change the world one day. Terry, LeAnn and I would cruise the main "street" of Grand Marais wearing LeAnn's cat eye glasses she bought at Ben Franklin for 99 cents. We didn't think we were cool...we KNEW we were cool. At the time Grand Marais was a lot like most small towns, one main street. There really wasn't much to see or do so we had to create our own entertainment. (I guess that explains the cat eye glasses huh?) The closest movie theater was Duluth, about 110 miles away so going to a movie was out of the question. Cable TV and VCR's were not even on the radar at the time and what in the world was MTV???.

Cruising often lead to parking by the lake and eating Dairy Queen. I don't mean that kind of "parking" although Terry might have enjoyed that as LeAnn and I were both a couple of "hotties"! The three of us would just talk and dream. Our conversations often turned to needing a place to hang out. This would be a place where we could all go, maybe play some video games and eat. The DQ was too small and the other restaurants in town didn't want a bunch of local kids hanging around making fun of the tourists. Terry took all of this to heart and changed Grand Marais forever when he and his brother Sid opened Sven and Ole's Pizza. If you've ever visited Grand Marais you've at least seen the bumper stickers and hopefully have tried this fantastic pizza.

The point of all this reminiscing is this: listen to the ideas of our youth, don't ever think "This is as good as it gets." Believe that change can be good because you never know what will come; You might get your name on a bumper sticker, invent a great pizza and give the kids a place to hang out!

My Favorite Sven and Ole Joke

Ole came home from work early, one day, don cha know, and he found Lena sitting there in their room naked with no clothes on. "Vat are you doing Lena?" he asked. "Oh, I just didn't have anything to wear." she said. Ole went over to the closet, and said "Vat do you mean, you have nothin' to wear. Look, you have a red dress, a green dress, a blue dress, "Hi Sven", a yellow dress...

Even if you can't have Sven and Ole's pizza where you live you can make your own very good pizza crust easily in the bread machine. Just set it on the dough only cycle and when it's ready you can bake it on a pizza stone or cookie sheet. My kids each take some dough and press it into their own pans for personal pan pizzas. Toppings can be anything from red sauce to Alfredo sauce, pepperoni to chicken and mushrooms to pineapple. I DO NOT, however, recommend the use of zucchini! (Yuck!)

Traditional Pizza Crust

¾ cup warm water
½ teaspoon salt
2 ½ cups bread flour
1 teaspoon sugar
2 teaspoons active dry yeast
1 Tablespoon cornmeal

Place all ingredients in bread pan in order directed by bread machine instruction manual. Program dough cycle setting; press start. Remove dough when cycle ends; let rest 5 minutes. Roll out dough to 14" circle. Use your favorite toppings and bake at 400 degrees for 15 minutes or until the crust is nicely browned.

Olive Oil Pizza Crust

½ cup water
¾ teaspoon salt
2 Tablespoons olive oil
2 ½ cups flour
2 teaspoons sugar
2 teaspoons active dry yeast

Measure all ingredients into the bread machine pan. Select the dough setting. Press Start. When the unit signals and display reads 0:00 press Stop and remove dough. Pat dough into 12 by 15 inch rimmed baking sheet or a greased 12 inch round pizza pan. Let stand for 10 minutes. Preheat oven to 400 degrees. Spread pizza sauce over dough, add desired toppings and bake 15 to 20 minutes, or until crust is golden brown. I also like to put garlic powder in with the ingredients for a garlicky crust.

Garlic Herb Pizza Crust

1 cup warm water
3 Tablespoons olive oil
3 Tablespoons Sugar
1 teaspoon Salt
2 ½ cups flour
2 teaspoons minced garlic (dried or fresh)
2 ¼ teaspoons active dry yeast
½ teaspoon dried oregano
½ teaspoon dried basil leaves

Combine water, olive oil, sugar, salt in pan of bread machine Add flour, then sprinkle garlic on flour. Lastly add yeast. Turn machine on dough cycle. As the dough mixes, sprinkle in oregano and basil until it suits you for color and taste. Let mix for about 15 to 30 minutes. Let the dough rest from 5 to 30 minutes. The longer it rests, the thicker and more tasty the crust. Meanwhile, preheat oven to 475 degrees. Roll out dough on a lightly floured surface. Spray a large pizza pan with nonstick cooking spray. Place dough on pan and add your choice of pizza toppings. Bake in preheated oven until golden brown, about 12 to 15 minutes.

(Gulp) It's Zucchini Season
– Lock your cars!

The pressure has been unrelenting...actually only my sweet neighbor has even mentioned it and handed me a couple of recipes, but I'll cave in any way for her sake. Zucchini recipes! Here they are.

I feel I must go back and give you a little history on my aversion to this vegetable. Let's blame it on my mother. She grew up in the time when nothing, I repeat, nothing was wasted. Even if you didn't like it, you cooked it and passed it off onto your children disguised as dinner. To call my mother thrifty would be an understatement. We rarely bought paper towels and if we did you tore them in half to conserve. She used rags. We had a rag bag by the dryer where my mom would keep old T-shirts and Dad's flannel work shirts with the buttons cut off. These rags were used for everything from dusting to washing the floor.

She also liked to sew additional fabric to the bottom of our jeans so we could get an extra few months out of them after we had a growth spurt. Any bar soap we bought was taken from its wrapper and set out to dry because we all know hard soap lasts longer than soft soap. And on the rare occasions any pop was purchased it was the Holiday gas station brand (10 cans for a buck) and we had to open it with a can key. We had never heard of a pop top can?

The one place my mom didn't try to conserve money was unfortunately on the electricity of her iron. Why she chose this as her "splurge" is beyond me. She ironed everything! (My iron has so much dust on it you'd think it hadn't been used in ten years....or longer.) "Go get me some hangers" was her favorite way to interrupt Saturday morning cartoons. She even ironed my Dad's bandana hankies. I can guarantee that if my Dad had his pockets searched today you would find a red or blue bandana hankie in there.

Back to zucchini, my mom didn't grow it as I remember, she got it the way most people do…someone dumped a bag on our front step while we were at the laundromat. She just couldn't throw it on the leaf pile as it was after all, food. So she dug out her cookbooks and decided to serve it to us straight up, which is to say with the name zucchini right in the title, Zucchini Bread. There lies her critical mistake. My brother and I wouldn't touch it. Bread should not have vegetables in it. Bananas sure! Not zucchini! When that tactic failed her she tried the sneaky approach, grated into spaghetti sauce. Yuck!!! Then outright put it into food we didn't like anyway like Swiss steak with zucchini and cooked tomatoes. (Could there be a more vile concoction?)

I have tried my best to bring you three of the *least* abhorrent recipes I could find containing zucchini. I will be honest with you these recipes HAVE NOT been pre tested in my kitchen. I just couldn't do it. If you don't like the results it's your own fault for cooking with zucchini in the first place. One neighbor had the best idea. Let the kids make boats out of the zucchini and send it down the river. Bye Bye Zucchini.

> *"The first zucchini I ever saw I killed it with a hoe."*
> John Gould, 'Monstrous Depravity' 1963.

Beef Stuffed Zucchini

1 ½ pounds uncooked lean ground beef
1 large onion, chopped
1 large green pepper, chopped
1 ¼ cups soft breadcrumbs
1 egg, beaten
1 Tablespoon dried parsley

1 teaspoon basil
1 teaspoon Italian seasoning
1 teaspoon salt
⅛ teaspoon pepper
16 ounces canned tomato sauce, divided
2 medium tomatoes, chopped
5 medium zucchini
2 cups mozzarella cheese, shredded

In a large bowl, combine the first 11 ingredients and 8 ounces of tomato sauce; mix well. Stir in tomatoes. Halve zucchini lengthwise; scoop out seeds. Fill with meat mixture; place in two 13 x 9 inch baking dishes. Spoon remaining tomato sauce over each. Bake uncovered at 375 degrees for 45 minutes or until zucchini is tender. Sprinkle with cheese the last 4 minutes of baking.

Zucchini & Potatoes Au Gratin

3 cups potatoes, peeled and cooked
3 cups zucchini, sliced (one half inch)
2 Tablespoons water
3 Tablespoons butter
3 Tablespoons flour
1 Tablespoon chicken bouillon granules
1 ½ cups milk
1 cup cheddar cheese, shredded
2 Tablespoons pimento, chopped
½ teaspoon thyme
1 cup French fried onions

Preheat oven to 350 degrees.

In a medium saucepan cook the zucchini in the water for 5 minutes or until just tender; drain and set aside. Melt butter in the saucepan, add flour and bouillon granules. Gradually stir in milk; cooking until sauce is thick and smooth. Remove sauce from heat, stir in cheese, pimento and thyme; keep stirring until cheese melts. In a medium greased casserole dish, layer ½ of the potatoes, zucchini and then sauce. Repeat layers ending with sauce. Bake uncovered for 20 to 30 minutes until casserole is bubbly and heated through. Sprinkle with French fried onions to cover and bake an additional 2 or 3 minutes to warm.

Super Zucchini Casserole

3 cups sliced zucchini
8 ounces package stuffing, prepared as directed
⅛ cup onion
1 cup grated carrots
1 cup sour cream
4 Tablespoons butter or margarine
1 can cream of chicken soup

Preheat oven to 350 degrees.

Sauté zucchini and onions until tender in butter, about 30 minutes. Fold in sour cream, carrots and soup. Pour into baking dish, top with stuffing and bake for 30 minutes.

Grandma Elsie, Planting the Seeds of Youth

My sister-cousin's family had a big TO-DO when the family matriarch, Grandma Elsie, celebrated her 102nd birthday. I know you're probably picturing a family surrounding a sweet little lady being wheeled around a nursing home eating pureed birthday cake, but that is truly not the case. Elsie lives in her little one bedroom house she has called home since 1960. She shops for herself once a week when her son, who's 79, takes her to grocery store. She cooks and cleans for herself, with some assistance of a cleaning lady, but that is a luxury of the recent years. She still insists she do her own laundry. Elsie has relied on each of her seven sons or public transportation to drive her here and there for the past 67 years since her husband Abner died, as she never held a drivers license.

On this day to celebrate her birthday she walked right into my sister-cousin's house and had a steaming bowl of homemade chicken noodle soup. No huge fuss as they had a big party at the church for just a year ago on her 101st .birthday.

It is fun to talk with her and her children about their childhood memories. She had a horse she rode to school and she loved to ski. All of her kids spoke only Norwegian at home and didn't learn to speak English until they attended school. Her children were all born at home. One baby came when it was winter and very cold. The doctor was so drunk when he showed up he could hardly deliver the baby. They found the doctor stone cold dead in a ditch the very next day. He passed out on his way home and froze to death. One son remembered their first car. It was a Chevy bought in 1935. Grandpa ran over one sons foot as he backed it out of the garage. They had no money as the Great Depression had hit them hard. When the bank came to repossess the car they couldn't find it. Abner had removed all the tires and put it up on blocks and hid it. There was no way they could get it back then.

My son Ben was telling my mom that Grandma Elsie grows some flowers in her garden that keep her young. I was confused by where he had gotten this idea until I realized he was switching around a conversation I had earlier. I had told him that caring for her garden probably keeps her young. But in thinking about it now, little Ben had it right all along. Every time Elsie plants a seed, be it flower or vegetable, she is bringing forth a life and in caring for that life it gives her responsibility. It is in that responsibility of caring, nurturing and cultivating she finds her own youth. It's a simple motto "use it or lose it" whether it be gardening or doing whatever you love and Elsie is a perfect example of a lady who knows how to use it well.

I would love to share with you some of her recipes but her sons laugh that she wasn't a very good cook, just a great mom. Let's go with a Norwegian theme in honor of her heritage. Sorry no Lutefisk recipes though. I'm allergic.

Norwegian Oatmeal Lace Cookies

½ cup butter
1 ½ cups regular rolled oats
1 egg
⅔ cup sugar
1 teaspoon baking powder
1 Tablespoon flour

Melt the butter in a small saucepan and stir in the oatmeal. Beat egg until foamy with the sugar. Mix together the baking powder and flour and stir into the egg mixture along with the oatmeal mixture.

Drop batter, 1 level Tablespoon at a time, onto greased and floured baking sheets, 2 to 3 inches apart.

Bake at 375 degrees for 10 minutes or until golden brown. Place baking sheets on wire racks to cool, about 1 minute (cookies should still be hot and flexible, but cooled until firm enough to move). Quickly lift cookies with a spatula; drape them over a horizontal broomstick covered with foil; press gently into saddle shape. (If cookies harden and stick to pan, return to oven until softened.) When cool, lift off broomstick. Store airtight at room temperature 2 or 3 days; freeze for longer storage. Makes about 2 dozen.

Almond Nut Cake

4 eggs
¾ cup sugar
1 teaspoon baking powder
2 cups ground almonds or other nuts

Preheat the oven to 350 degrees. Beat eggs and sugar until light and lemon-colored. Combine baking powder and nuts and fold carefully into the egg mixture. Pour into a greased 9 inch spring-form pan. Bake 30 minutes. Cool in the pan. Serve with whipped cream or ice cream.

Norwegian Lemon Bon Bons

1 cup butter
⅓ cup powder sugar
¾ cup corn starch
1 cup flour
½ cup finely chopped pecans
Juice of one half a lemon

Sandy Holthaus

Blend butter and sugar, add corn starch and flour. Chill dough until manageable. Roll into balls. Spread chopped pecans on waxed paper and sprinkle with a Tablespoon of powdered sugar. Place the balls on the nuts and press with the bottom of a glass. Bake nut side up on a cookie sheet at 350 degrees for 15 minutes. When cool frost with a mixture of one cup powdered sugar, lemon juice and one Tablespoon of melted butter.

The Power of the Pull

It is known by some that I have a younger brother. I guess you could say that he is almost my twin as we are only ten months apart and because of how our birthdays fell on the calendar we were put into the same grade at school. He is much taller, blonde, and by all definitions, physically stronger than me. An asset you say??? Well possibly now, as adults, if I need him to sling a few bales of hay his brute strength would come in handy. But as children, not so much. The power that comes from being physically stronger than your older sister was HUGE. He could carry more wood, therefore filling his side of the rick faster. He could pin me down until I agreed to let him pick which T. V. show we were going to watch. (We only had one T. V. so I had to slug it out if I wanted to watch the John Denver Christmas Special.) But most frustrating of all – he could start the snowmobile and I couldn't even give it a pull.

My parents bought two Polaris snowmobiles when we were about eight. Our property backed up to a highline. This is a wide open field where the huge power lines ran through for miles and miles. Perfect for dirt bikes in the summer and snowmobiles in the winter. My dad's policy back then was: "Don't ride any further than you can walk." My problem was sometimes I would get the snowmobile stuck and kill it. Since I couldn't pull the starter myself I had to negotiate with my much stronger, younger, brother to help me. It was either that or walk home. He kept a laundry list of chores that I could do for him if he started my sled; from dishes to vacuuming to making his bed…. and depending on the weather and how far from home we were the price could go as high as FOLDING CLOTHES! It was sheer torture.

I distinctly remember the *exact* day everything changed. I

was really, really far from home and my snow machine had died. It was just starting to snow and it looked like I had a miserable walk home ahead of me when my brother pulled up with that grin on his face. You ALL know the grin I'm talking about. The "Sandy you will be cleaning my room for a month" grin. I was so mad; no begging would get him to help me unless I gave in to his demands. I dug in my heels and pulled at that cord with everything I had….and…it…started. Just like that. The look of surprise on his face was worth a week of dishes. The freedom I felt was fantastic! And strange as it seems once I had started the snowmobile that day I knew I could start it every time from then on. IN-DE-PEND-ENCE – Yeah! I had the power of the pull, well, when it came to the snowmobile anyway, the T.V. was a different story. I finally gave it up and became a reader. I guess I should thank him for that. Thanks Bro!

> *"Life is 10 percent what happens to you and 90*
> *percent how you react to it. " ~ Lou Holtz*

The power of the pull also comes from a super breakfast. Here are some great ideas to start your day with plenty of fuel to pull you through.

Oatmeal Crunch Breakfast Bars

4 cups quick cooking rolled oats
1 ½ cups chopped walnuts
1 cup packed brown sugar
1 cup coconut
1 teaspoon salt
¾ cup butter
¾ cup orange marmalade OR ¾ cup Nutella
(One will give you a fruit flavor the other chocolate)

Combine all ingredients and press into a 15 by 10 jellyroll pan.

(This is a cookie sheet with sides.) Bake at 400 degrees for 18 to 22 minutes or until golden brown.

Brain Shakes – from my Sister-Cousin Dawn Sorensen

2 cups vanilla, plain or strawberry yogurt. (If you choose to use a plain yogurt add one or two teaspoons of honey to the recipe.)
1 cup fresh or frozen blueberries
¼ cup flax seed meal
1 banana

Place all in a blender. Whip until smooth. A perfect way to start your day.

Cinnamon Crunch Pull-Apart Muffins

¼ cup chopped pecans
⅔ cup sugar
1 ½ teaspoon cinnamon
1 ½ teaspoon nutmeg
½ cup butter, melted
1 Tablespoon flour
Two packages refrigerator biscuits.

Preheat oven to 375 degrees. Combine pecans, sugar and spices in a bowl. Mix well. Cut each biscuit into four pieces. Dip biscuit into melted butter then into sugar pecan mixture. Divide into twelve muffin cups (about five or six pieces in each) Add flour and melted butter to the remaining sugar pecan mixture and spoon evenly over each muffin cup. Bake 20 to 25 minutes or until muffins are golden brown. Cool about five minutes and serve warm.

Everyone should have a BFF
(Big Farmer Friend)

I have a BFF. He shoots straight from the hip and I know he reads this column because he comments on it frequently. I usually trust his judgment. (He didn't like a Noxzema column I wrote and I respect that.) But I must tell you I think he seriously missed the mark awhile back and I was completely baffled. Here's the story. My BFF stopped me and said "I think you have too many irons in the fire." I was puzzled by this. I mean I appreciate his concern but I thought I juggled wife, daughter, mother, cook, bottle washer, maid, alpaca farmer, small business owner, writer, school volunteer (….all roles I love by the way) quite well. Where had I gone wrong? Had I shown a weakness of some kind somewhere? Had he secretly seen my messy closets? No, not possible.

Then it hit me as I was driving home…."Ah yes, of course, **he's a man.**" It would be only natural of him to assume I had too many balls in the air as most men are not good jugglers. (Now don't argue with me fellas it's a scientific fact, err OK ask any woman and she will tell you, men can't handle more than one thing at a time.) Case and point: When has George Bush (President) ever driven his minivan (Chauffer) to pick up his wife Laura's dry cleaning (Husband/Maid) while talking to his mom Barbara on his cell phone (Son) with three screaming children in the backseat (Father) all wanting Happy Meals? (Caterer) The answer is: Never! Yet I could give you the names of ten women who would say, that was their morning.

It's called multi – tasking and I know it's a big word so let me break it down. Women have these wonderful brains that are like a pound of ground beef. Versatile, flexible and 101 Uses. Cook us up and the possibilities are endless. Don't get me wrong, I love men dearly; I just know it's best not to throw too much information at them all at once, especially let's say, while they are watching football. Here is what they hear: I need....can you.....did you know......dinner....please turn off stove.....SCORE!

I truly believe most women would LOVE to have the ability to only think about one thing at a time. (Compartmentalized thinking – yes there is a name for it.) But unfortunately, our brains won't let it happened. (Don't argue with me guys because again, it's a scientific fact, we have done the studies!) We want to watch a Lifetime movie uninterrupted but we actually HEAR the kids jumping off the furniture in the basement and we HAVE to check it out. We can't tune it out. No way - no how.

This all reminds me of an old joke. There was a brain surgeon who was selling used brains for transplantation. The women's brains cost $500.00 while a man's brains was selling for $10,000.00. The men were smug and laughing until the surgeon explained the men's brains were worth more because "they were hardly ever used". Cracks me up every time!

So my dear BFF I really truly appreciate your very genuine the concern but let's face it I am only using about one tenth of by brain at this time and I could seriously use a new challenge!

Here are five of the 101 Uses for a Pound of ground Beef – Enjoy!

This is the easiest way to brown a pound of hamburger if you have to hit the ground running in the morning. Place one pound of frozen ground beef in the crock pot. (Yes guys you have to remove the wrapper first.) Dissolve one beef bouillon cup into a half cup of hot water and add it to the hamburger. After 8 hours on low or 4 hours on high you will have fully browned pound of ground beef. Mash with a fork and use any of the following options for a quick and easy dinner in minutes.

Goulash

Add three cups cooked elbow macaroni and one can tomato soup.
Stir and heat through. I add about one fourth cup shredded cheddar cheese to the top and cover the crock pot for a few minutes until melted.

Stroganoff

Add three cups cooked noodles, one can of sliced mushrooms (drained) one can cream of mushroom soup, one half cup of sour cream, garlic salt to taste and one teaspoon dried parsley over the top before serving.

Chili

Add once can each, chili beans, kidney beans, pork and beans, crushed tomatoes and tomato paste. Add one teaspoon garlic powder and chili powder to taste. Mix well warm through and serve.

Shepards Pie

Add one cup frozen veggies and one can cream of mushroom soup. Stir well and transfer to a 9 by 9 inch baking pan. Dollop with mashed potatoes (instant is OK) and heat in oven at 350 degrees until potatoes are golden brown.

Made-Rites (Sloppy Joes)

Add one can of tomato soup, one half cup ketchup, one Tablespoon yellow mustard and one fourth cup brown sugar. Stir well and serve on buns.

Best Friends, Bacon and Boys
A Perfect Winters Day

When I was in fifth grade I had the best of best friends. She was in the sixth grade and had two older sisters so she was a wealth of girl knowledge and information. She knew all there was to know about boys. She taught me that if you were mean to boys and pretended you didn't like them they would really like you back. She was mean to lots of boys so she was pretty popular. We had crushes on two new brothers who had moved to Taconite Harbor. Their dad worked for the forestry and they both had really long hair. (Something the local boys did not do at the time.) She liked the boy in fifth grade and I liked the boy in sixth grade so we each spied on the other ones crush in class every day. Nights were spent on the phone comparing notes. One day she got me a class picture of the boy I liked. I still have that photo to this day in my Bible under Matthew 10. (His name and his age.) It was destiny. We were to be married and have at least six long haired children.

She and I were together almost every weekend doing one of two things: either listening to Jackson Browne's Running on Empty album or starting fires in the woods. These fires were great. We didn't build huge bon fires but instead made little tiny stick fires we covered with a metal coffee can. This was our grill. Here's how it worked, we would take a key type can opener and punch holes around the outside edges so the fire could get air then we would put the can upside down over the tiny fire and cook bacon on the top which was really the bottom of the can. Bacon in the woods on a cold winter's day is like nothing you've ever ordered at the finest restaurant. We would pretend to be pioneers cooking up our last hog just to survive in the tundra. It makes my tummy growl just to think of it now.

One day while we were enjoying a cookout near the Temperance River when we heard shouts of laughter and screams. We went to investigate and almost died. It was our two crushes with their whole family tobogganing down the unplowed Temperance River road. They invited us to join them! It was SO MUCH FUN! Their dad was really funny as he explained the complicated rules of tobogganing. When he leaned right, lean right. When he leaned left, lean left and when he bailed off you could choose to jump off with him or go for it all the way to the bottom. We soon learned that he liked to jump off early so he didn't have to pull the sled back up the hill. Tobogganing is also better than regular sledding because you all ride together. Their toboggan held six people so the odds of one of us riding next to the boy we liked were very high! We burned up the phone lines that night with details of them holding our hands to help us up out of the snow banks or pulling us up the hill to show us how strong they were. We just knew there would be a double wedding with bacon appetizers!

"First love is a little foolish and a lot of curiosity."- George Bernard Shaw

Rumaki
(Bacon wrapped Water Chestnuts and Chicken Livers)

1 pound bacon cut in half
1 pound chicken livers cut in half
2 cans water chestnuts (whole)
1 bottle of teriyaki sauce
toothpicks

Preheat oven to 375 degrees. Open and drain water chestnuts, place in small bowl, cut chicken livers in half and place with the water chestnuts. Pour teriyaki sauce over water chestnuts and chicken, just enough to cover. Let marinate for about 1 to 2 hours in the refrigerator. After marinating wrap one slice of bacon around one whole chestnut and one chicken liver. Hold bacon in place with a toothpick. Place on baking sheet and bake until bacon is crispy, about 20 to 25 minutes. Serve warm.

Spiced Bacon Bites

Bacon is cooked with sugar and cinnamon coating, a tasty appetizer recipe.

1 pound bacon, thick-sliced, room temperature
1 ¼ cups brown sugar
2 teaspoons cinnamon

Cut each slice of bacon in half, crosswise. Mix sugar and cinnamon together and thoroughly coat each slice of bacon. Twist slices or leave flat, and place on rack in broiler or jellyroll pan in a 350 degree oven.

Bake until bacon is crisp and sugar is bubbly, 15 to 20 minutes. The sugar can burn quickly, so watch closely. Let cool and serve at room temperature. Makes 16 to 20 appetizer servings.

Hot Bacon Appetizers

½ pound bacon, cooked and crumbled
¾ cup shredded cheddar cheese
¼ cup butter, softened
2 teaspoons caraway seeds
50 Melba toast rounds or a loaf of party rye bread

Combine first 4 ingredients, mixing well. Spread evenly on toast rounds or party rye. Place on baking sheet and broil 2 minutes or until cheese melts. Serve hot. Yield: 50 appetizers.

Remembering Grandma Elpert
(January 2008)

Great Grandma Margaret holding Jack
Louis in her kitchen Spring 1999

Over the holidays our family sadly lost Grandma Margaret. (Great Grandma to my children.) She was 91 years old. At her wake lots of comments were made to try to soothe our sad hearts. "She had a long life...." She's with Louie (her husband) now.... Heaven has a new angel...." Sweet and kind as these words are, they bring no comfort to me. I am selfish. I want her here. It just breaks my heart to think of her gone. I have tears in my eyes and a catch in my throat as I type these words. I can say to you without a doubt she was the loveliest woman I ever met. In the 14 years that I knew her she never raised her voice or said an unkind word to or about anyone. When I close my eyes I can still see her smiling face and hear her soft chuckle.

She was especially kind and sweet to all of her great grandchildren. The oldest grandson, Blake, would spend time with her after school each day until his parents came home from work. The two would play cards together. Blake sent her to heaven with a deck of cards in her hands. Our son Jack Louis was named after her husband Louie and I swear her eyes would light up just at the mention of her dear husband's name. I believe Jack held a special place in her heart just because of his namesake. I pray that each of the great grandchildren remember her forever.

Grandma Margaret was well known for her baking. A few years ago Zoë and I put together a handmade cookbook of all her recipes for the family as a Christmas present. Everyone had a favorite recipe they wanted in the book. Without a doubt I loved her Texas Cake Bars. I had to stop making them because I gained weight just smelling them bake. Her cookies were the best. She made frosted buttermilk sugar cookies, chocolate chip cookies, monster cookies and several more. All were perfect. I am not exaggerating. Every cookie was the EXACT same shape and size. She would stack them neatly in these elongated baggies and freeze them. No one left her house without a baggie of cookies. My brother in law, Mark saved the sugar cookies he received more than five years before her death when she moved from her home to the assisted living center. He placed them on a plate at her wake with a sign that read "Grandma's Last Batch of Cookies." People cried, yet nodded in remembrance. We worried someone would eat one.

After the wake her grandchildren, one of which is my husband Michael, got together to talk about Grandma and their favorite memories of her. I was surprised by some of the stories. I never knew that Grandma had learned to drive and got a drivers license in her 60's. I did know she kept a perfect lawn and she was an immaculate housekeeper. I did not know she made the best buttered toast in the world. (More than one grandchild attested to that.) I did know she love to fish, watch sports and play a good game of Euchre. I started to think about how I live my life and wondered what will I be remembered for when I am gone. Wouldn't we all be better people if we lived according to the question…"What will they say at my eulogy?" …...

"People may not remember exactly what you did, or what you said, but they will always remember how you made them feel." ~ Someone very wise

Texas Cake Bars – Grandma Margaret Elpert

2 cups sugar
2 cups flour
2 sticks butter
4 Tablespoons cocoa
1 teaspoon vanilla
1 cup water
½ cup buttermilk
1 teaspoon baking soda
2 eggs – beaten

Sift sugar and flour into a bowl. Combine butter, cocoa and water into a saucepan and bring to a boil. Pour the cocoa mixture over the flour – sugar mixture. Add the remaining ingredients and mix well. Pour onto buttered jellyroll pan. Bake at 400 degrees for 20 to 25 minutes. Cool and frost.

Texas Cake Bar Frosting

1 stick butter
5 to 6 Tablespoons of milk (do not use cream)
1 teaspoon vanilla
4 Tablespoons cocoa
1 pound powdered sugar

Combine butter, milk and cocoa in a saucepan. Bring to a boil and let cool. Add powdered sugar and vanilla. Beat well then spread on cooled bars.

Frosted Buttermilk Sugar Cookies – Grandma Margaret Elpert

2 cups sugar
2 eggs
1 cup buttermilk
2 teaspoons soda
1 cup lard or shortening
2 teaspoons vanilla
3 to 4 cups flour
½ teaspoon salt

Mix all ingredients well. Chill dough. Roll out on floured surface to one half an inch thick. Cut with large cookie cutter and bake until golden brown around the edges. Then ice with powdered sugar frosting.

Powdered Sugar Frosting

1 pound powdered sugar
3 Tablespoons softened butter
1 Tablespoon milk
1 teaspoon vanilla
A dash of salt

Beat well until creamy. Color if you wish. Frost cookies.

We've Gone to the Dogs!

Ben Michael and his dachshund puppy Maggie May in 2009

Don't ask me why we did it or how it happened, the stories will differ depending on which Holthaus you interview, but we purchased another puppy bringing our family dog total to four. All I remember is a family vote where we discussed democracy and the next thing I knew our youngest son Ben had a Doxie. Maggie May is now three months old and not a bundle of joy! Sure she's cute and that alone will buy her some extra points. She's also smart as a whip but yet hasn't figured out that the great outdoors makes a wonderful commode compared to that of the living room carpet. She has a great nose and likes laundry and trash. Both of which she strews about the house at her convenience.

What were we thinking??? Four indoor dogs and one very

lovely home do not go hand in hand. My mother says that you must vacuum at least once a week for each person and pet in the home, people that means counting the cats I must vacuum our house ten times a week! Am I to squeeze it in twice on Mondays, Wednesdays and Fridays??? I have yet to figure that out.

I love dogs! I really do, but there were much firmer rules with the dogs I grew up with as a child. We had linoleum floors in the kitchen and dining areas and that was the ONLY place the dogs were allowed. I remember them resting their heads on the edge of the living room carpet while we watched T.V. in the evening but they never dared to enter the room. As far as dogs in the bedroom or "God Forbid" on the beds you might as well have said you had a UFO in your room. Now I'm Ellie Clampett with three dogs tucked in my bed here or there all night long. (We have a fat one who can't make the jump onto the bed so she snores on the floor all through the night!)

All of our pets are great company and very loyal. There is no sneaking up to our door. They hear you just making plans to stop over and they will bark at every imagined threat throughout the day. (Just ask UPS man and Schwann's man as they have been licked to death at our house more than once.)

When I took Maggie May to the vet in Kimball last week he fell in love. He asked me a theoretical question...If I could start all over with my fiancé and I was offered a huge diamond ring or this lovely little puppy which would I choose? I think he was a bit disappointed when I quickly chose the ring, but then again she doesn't drag his underwear around the house now does she?

Here is my favorite Dog joke....try to read it with an Irish accent....

A farmer named Muldoon lived alone in the Irish countryside with a pet dog he doted on. The dog died and Muldoon went to the parish priest and asked, "Father, me dog is dead. Could you be saying a mass for the creature?"

Father Patrick replied, "No, we cannot have services for an animal in the church, but there's a new denomination down the road, no telling what they believe, but maybe they'll do something for the animal."

Muldoon said, "I'll go right now Father. Do ye think $5,000 is enough to donate for the service?"

To which Father Patrick replied, "Eh, Muldoon, why didn't you tell me the dog was Catholic!"

Hush Puppies

2 cups self-rising cornmeal mix
¾ cup milk
1 egg, beaten
1 onion, chopped finely
¼ teaspoon garlic salt

Combine cornmeal mix, milk, egg, and onion; mix well. Drop by rounded teaspoons into deep hot oil (375 degrees), frying only a few at a time until golden brown. Test the first ones cooked. Adjust the amount of batter used or the oil temperature until hush puppies are brown and done. Drain on absorbent paper. Makes about 2 dozen puppies.

Hot Dogs and Noodles

1 pound hot dogs, cut into chunks
3 cans tomato soup
1 Tablespoon dried onion flakes
dash hot sauce
1 pound bow tie noodles
1 (8 ounce) package shredded cheddar cheese

Heat hot dogs, tomato soup, onion flakes and hot sauce. Prepare bow tie noodles. Preheat oven to 375. Place noodles in baking pan. Pour sauce mixture over and stir. Sprinkle cheese over top; place in oven until cheese melts (approximately 5 to 10 minutes).

Easy Hot Dogs on the Go

I like to take hot dogs to the park or to ball games on the summer. This is the easiest way to go. Place one or two packs of hot dogs in a beverage cooler or thermos. Cover with boiling water and screw the lid on tight. Just pack tongs, buns and ketchup. The hot dogs will be ready when you are!

Batter Up

I love batter. As a child I would beg my mother to let me bake crazy cakes just so I could eat spoonful after spoonful of the batter before putting the cake into the oven. (Sometime even after it was in the oven I would sneak a few more spoonfuls before the batter got too hot.) Crazy cake is made without eggs so the argument that raw eggs would make me sick was out, mom had to revert to the old "Because I said not to eat it, that's why" spiel. It didn't matter if the batter was chocolate, yellow, spice or brownie, I ate them all. My dad had a huge sweet tooth so he loved all the cake in the house. If it wasn't frosted he didn't care, he would just cut his piece in half and put butter in the middle and eat it that way. I didn't really like the cake once it was baked. The batter was much more appealing.

I thought I was the only one with a batter eating fetish until I met a lady at work. During a communication seminar, each person had to share their most embarrassing moment. Her story went like this…..she was mixing up cake batter in a bowl using a hand held electric mixer, the cord came unplugged and landed right in the batter. No one was looking so she fished the cord out of the batter and stuck it in her mouth…..completely forgetting that the other end was still plugged into the wall! She received the shock of her life and then had to explain to her husband why she stuck an electrical cord in her mouth just to retrieve a little bit of batter. I laughed really loud as I could actually SEE myself committing the same batter-cide one day. I asked her if this shock therapy had cured her of her batter cravings, she said no. I guess it takes more than a few volts to cure this "disease".

I am afraid I have passed this gene onto my daughter and her friends, although for them it's raw cookie dough. They will make up a batch of chocolate chip cookie dough at 2 A.M. then eat most of the batch while watching scary movies. I've decided not to fight it as my mother did when I was young. Half the fun of being a kid is eating things that are bad for you. All those times she told me I would get a stomach ache or sick just never happened. Maybe it's just a mothers myth like sitting too close to the TV will ruin your eyes or cracking you knuckles will give you arthritis. Bad eyes and sore hands seem to just come with age...or do they???? You only live once....I'm willing to risk it...Batter up!

"Forty is the old age of youth; fifty the youth of old age." ~ Unknown

Here are three recipes that are easy for both kids and grownups to make. (And the batters are just delicious!)

Chocolate or Mocha Crazy Cake

3 cups flour
2 cups sugar
2 teaspoons soda
⅓ cup cocoa
Pinch salt
¾ cup salad oil
2 Tablespoons vinegar
1 teaspoon vanilla
2 cups water OR 2 cups cold coffee for Mocha Crazy Cake

Mix dry ingredients, then add remaining ingredients and beat until smooth. Bake in one 9 x 13 inch or two 8 inch round greased and floured pan(s) at 350 degrees for 40 to 45 minutes.

Easy Pound Cake

2 ¾ cups flour
2 teaspoons baking powder

1 teaspoon salt
1 ¾ cups sugar
1 cup butter
1 teaspoon vanilla
¾ cup milk

Combine all ingredients and add four eggs. Bake in bread pan at 375 degrees for 30 to 35 minutes. Cut like bread.

Peanut Butter Cupcakes

1 package yellow cake mix
2 eggs
⅓ cup oil
1 ¼ cups water
3 Tablespoons creamy peanut butter

Mix all ingredients until smooth; pour batter in paper lined tin. Bake at 350 degrees Make frosting while the cupcakes cool.

Frosting:
1 cup chocolate syrup
1 cup creamy peanut butter

Blend until smooth. Frost cupcakes.

4th of July a Time to Celebrate Our Freedom!

Growing up I loved the Fourth of July celebration held in Tofte just six miles from my home in Schroeder. Summer vacation would have just began to be boring as we had been out of school for about a month and most of us hadn't seen each other since the last day of school. Driving for "play dates" was <u>unheard of</u> at my house. I was thinking about this just last week as I was driving my daughter to her friend's house in Clearwater. FYI - a trip to Clearwater is 21 miles from our house in South Haven. So for my darling daughter to spend a day with her friend I must drive a total of 84 miles. Let's do the math together...my van gets 26 MPG and gas is about $3.00 per gallon so the total cost is about $9.69! Though some would consider this a small price to pay for a day of peace and quiet.....my mother wouldn't have driven me 84 miles for a blood transfusion; OK I exaggerate, maybe a BLOOD TRANSFUSION, but certainly not for day of backyard tanning and IPOD downloads! We played with the neighbor kids or we played alone. Period. I usually spent the summer with lots of books from the bookmobile. Even now I spend most of my summer vacation at the cabin reading a book a day. Some call it entertainment. I call it escapism.

If you have ever been to Tofte, MN you will notice an old road the runs along the lake below Highway 61. This is where they have the 4th of July parade every year. You could either watch the parade from the sidelines or throw a few streamers on your bike and be a part of it. If you were lucky you might get a spot on the fire truck and ride through the street from the top of the truck. One neighbor always had a classic car that he would bring to

Tofte for the day. Some people dressed silly as clowns or bums while others honored the day with military flags and colors.

It was a great day of good food; hay dances, and of course kids messing with fireworks. This was the loud, explosive, now banned in our fair state, bottle rocket, and firecracker kind of fireworks. I was probably about ten when I learned the very valuable lesson – don't light fire crackers while holding them in your hand. (In case you didn't know my friends, some fuses are shorter than others and you just might not have time to throw it before it explodes.) Two fears took over me when one blew up unexpectedly in between my fingers. One: – Will I still have fingertips? (Yes.) And Two: – Will my mother kill me? (Yes.) Kill might be a strong use of the word, but she did say that wasn't a very smart thing to do and she really had no sympathy for my charred fingers as they ached over the next week or two. (Mom also took the lighter away so I couldn't do any further damage to myself.) My dad was a "learn by your mistakes" kind of guy. I think he actually chuckled.

The best part of 4th of July was bringing your blankets and bug spray down to Lake Superior and watching the fireworks display in the night sky reflecting over the water. Tofte is well known for their beautiful and long fireworks show. People come for miles to literally "ooohh" and "aaahhh" over the dancing colors and explosions. If you sat downwind from where they lit the fuses the smoke would keep the mosquitoes to a dull hum and the slapping of pesky insects to a minimum.

My darling sister-cousin and I have made the trip back up north with our kids over the years and still enjoy this small town celebration of the independence of our country. Of course now the Annandale festivities rival the Tofte celebration as my kids like to spend the day with their friends, even though their mother is crazy enough to drive them around to their friends all summer long! A small price to pay for a little peace and quiet.

> *"This nation will remain the land of the free only*
> *so long as it is the home of the brave."*
> *~Elmer Davis*

Great Summer Salads and a to die for French dressing!! These are all super to take to barbeques and pot lucks. None are low cal though....Enjoy in moderation!

Carmel Apple Salad

1 medium can crushed pineapple (drain and save juice)
2 cups mini marshmallows
1 cup sugar
1 beaten egg
2 teaspoons corn starch
1 Tablespoon vinegar
4 large red apples (diced with skins on)
4 large green (Granny Smith) apples (diced with skins on)
1 (12 ounce) can skinless peanuts (not salt free)
2 large tubs of Cool Whip

Mix marshmallows and drained crushed pineapple in a small bowl, cover and refrigerate 3 hours or overnight. In a small saucepan, combine pineapple juice, beaten egg, sugar, cornstarch and vinegar, stirring and cooking on medium heat until thick. Cool and place in small bowl, refrigerate 3 hours or overnight. In a large mixing bowl, mix the above ingredients (after refrigerating specified time) with the apples, peanuts and whipped topping. Place in a large serving bowl and watch it disappear. It tastes just like a peanut covered caramel apple. Yield: 10 to 12 servings

Chicken Salad Croissants – Courtesy of the lovely Shannon Diers

2 cups cubed cooked chicken
1 cup cubed or shredded Swiss cheese
½ cup dill pickle relish
⅔ cup mayonnaise
1 Tablespoon minced fresh parsley
1 teaspoon lemon juice
½ teaspoon salt
⅛ teaspoon pepper

Lettuce leaves
Croissants

In a bowl, combine chicken, cheese and relish. Combine mayonnaise, parsley, lemon juice, salt & pepper; add to chicken mixture and mix well. Place a lettuce leaf on each croissant, top with about ½ cup of chicken mixture.

Just Like Tequilaberry's Salad

Salad Base:

One head of lettuce cut into bite size pieces
One head of cauliflower cut into bite size pieces
One and a half cup of parmesan cheese

Dressing:

1 cup of mayonnaise (not Miracle Whip)
¼ cup of sugar
¼ cup of milk
One pound of bacon fried crisp, drained and crumbled

Toss the two together and serve. (I think it is best to eat it all the first day as this salad tends to get watery the second day.)

Grandma Hart's French Dressing

2 cups sugar
Juice of 2 lemons
1 medium onion, chopped
1 cup salad oil (I use canola oil)
3 Tablespoons paprika
1 Tablespoon salt
1 cup ketchup
¾ cup vinegar

Place oil, vinegar and onions in the blender. When onions are liquefied add remaining ingredients. Bottle and refrigerate.

How Many is Too Many???

Last week my son Ben and I were pitching hay in the barn for the alpacas and to our surprise we pitched two babies bunnies! (They were not hurt, just startled as they had been cozily sleeping in the hay with seven other brothers and sisters.) Now in most barns this would seem odd but we have lots and lots of bunnies and they keep on coming. We started with two female rabbits. I got tired of cleaning their cages so one day I opened the door to the hutch and let them go. They didn't run away. The two of them just moseyed around the yard eating flowers and grass. It was cute to watch them from the kitchen window. Then I pushed my luck and bought a third rabbit at the Winneshiek County Fair in Iowa. It turns out he was a boy bunny....I guess you know the rest of the story. I did have the boy bunny fixed but it was too late, the dam was already broken only our flood was rabbits instead of water. Before you knew it we had at least forty bunnies running around the yard. The kids found 14 tiny rabbits in the barn last summer and we had a bunny sale. One man called and said he would take the lot but when I found out he planned to cook them up I just couldn't do it.

I was telling my mom this story and she said well "I guess you didn't learn your lesson." What lesson??? "Sandy, remember the mice?" Ohmygoodness! I had completely forgotten about the mice. When I was in fifth grade my parents let me buy two mice at the Miller Hill Mall in Duluth. They were two for a dollar. I decided to get two females so they *would not* have babies. Of course who knew they were both already expecting?? Before long I had a cage FULL of colorful crawling mice. One weekend we went out of town and I left the cage in an unfinished room upstairs. When we came home the cage was EMPTY! My mother had a fit! That meant the house had at least 50 mice running around. I was in tears because that meant we had to either poison them or trap them. My dad kept his cool and started looking around. He pulled a section of pink insulation off of the wall and started shaking it from the top. Wouldn't you know the mice came tumbling out! We scrambled to round them all up. That was the end of that. The next trip to Duluth I held a pail full of mice on my lap and we marched straight back to the pet shop. They had the choice to take them back or mom would let them go in the store. (She really wouldn't but the threat worked and they took them back. We didn't push for a refund.)

Well bunnies are not mice but they multiply very quickly. It is now a game when we come up our driveway to count them. A good friend gave us a bunny crossing sign last Christmas as a joke but it's actually true. They are constantly running across the driveway. If you would like a bunny and you don't plan to eat it stop by and take your pick!

I decided to include recipes that you start out eating just one cookie but quickly eat the whole batch! Sort of like rabbits – they sneak up on you and multiply. These are also all great recipes for the cookie exchanges coming up! I swear the Mounds Coconut Cookie recipe is so good you'll hide them! Enjoy!

Favorite bunny joke: A lady opened her refrigerator and saw a rabbit sitting on one of the shelves, "What are you doing in there?" she asked. The rabbit replied, "This is a Westinghouse, isn't it?" The lady confirmed, "Yes." "Well," the rabbit said, "I'm westing."

Mounds Coconut Cookies

⅓ cup butter
1 (3oz) package cream cheese, softened
¾ cup sugar
1 egg yolk
2 teaspoons almond or vanilla extract

2 teaspoons orange juice
1 ¼ cups flour
2 teaspoons baking powder
¼ teaspoon salt
5 cups flaked coconut
1 (9oz) package chocolate Kisses

In a large bowl cream together butter, cream cheese, and sugar. Add egg yolk and beat well. Add extract and orange juice. Mix together flour, baking powder, and salt. Add to butter mixture and mix well. Stir in 3 cups of coconut. Cover and chill at least an hour or overnight. Form the dough into one-inch balls. Roll in remaining coconut. Place on ungreased cookie sheet. Bake 10 to 12 minutes at 350 degrees. Check for light browning. Remove cookies to cooling rack. Press kiss in center of each one while the cookies are still warm.

Grandma Moulton's Sugar Cookies

1 cup sugar
1 cup powdered sugar
1 cup butter or margarine
1 cup cooking oil
2 eggs
4 ½ cups flour
1 teaspoon baking powder
1 teaspoon baking soda
1 teaspoon cream of tartar
1 teaspoon vanilla

Combine sugars, butter and oil, beat well. Add eggs and mix well. Add flour, baking powder, baking soda, cream of tartar and vanilla. Cover with plastic wrap and put in the refrigerator overnight. Make into small balls and flatten with the bottom of a glass or a cookie press. Take a brush with water and lightly brush the top of each cookie. Sprinkle with another layer of white sugar. (Or you can use colored sugar.) This will make a crackle coating on the top for an extra pretty look. Bake at 375 degrees for 10 to 12 minutes. Do not overcook.

Jam Thumbprint Cookies

⅔ cup butter
⅓ cup sugar
2 eggs, separated
½ teaspoon salt
1 ½ cups sifted flour
1 teaspoon vanilla
¾ cup walnuts
½ cup strawberry jam (Or use your favorite jam. I like tart jams like high bush cranberry or currant.)

Cream butter and sugar until fluffy. Add egg yolks, vanilla, salt. Beat. Gradually add flour. Shape into ¾ inch balls and dip in slightly beaten egg whites. Roll in walnuts. Place 1 inch apart on greased sheet. Press in middle with your thumb; bake five minutes at 350 degrees then add ¼ teaspoon jam in each thumb print. Bake at 350 degrees an additional ten minutes. Makes 3 dozen cookies.

Tis' Better to Give Than To Receive

Many people have asked me about the Christmas traditions my family shared when I was young. I hate to disappoint but my Christmas memories were not "Little House on the Prairie" with a fresh cut tree and "Pa" playing the fiddle. We had an artificial tree because my dad, like me, suffers from allergies. Real trees make us sneeze. So my children, too, are deprived of the fresh scent of pine. My mom would put the tree up in the bay window in the living room. We had these really cool snowball lights in all kinds of bright colors. We could buy them at them at Northland Hardware one at a time whenever we needed a replacement. I loved these bulbs because they had glitter all over them and they never got real hot like the other bulbs.

Christmas itself usually meant a really, really long car ride to visit both Grandparents. My Grandma Anderson lived in Onamia, MN and my Grandma and Grandpa Allard lived in Byron, MN. I can't begin to tell you how much I didn't like these trips. My dad smoked a pipe back then and he would go through a pack or two of Half and Half tobacco during the trip. My brother and I would die in the backseat begging him to crack a window before we got car sick. Sometimes he would get fed up with our complaining and play "freeze out". This is when he would roll down all the windows until we begged him to roll them up because our faces were frozen! I asked him once if he regretted smoking with us in the car when we were kids and he said no. "Everyone smoked back then." (I think he should regret it just a little bit don't you???)

When it came to buying gifts for my brother and me I think my parents were really smart. We didn't get tons of presents but we usually each had one special gift. In about third grade my mom ordered a bone china tea set from the Wards catalog. I still have that tea set to this day. Only one cup has been broken over the years. Another Christmas Santa gave me a Bentwood rocking chair and I am looking at it right now in my family room. I have a picture of me in that chair from more than 30 years ago. One gift I wish I had kept was my old record player. The kids recently found my old album collection. They called them "really big CD's". I decided to put a turntable in the family room so I could play them again.

All this reminiscing got me thinking recently which gifts will stand the test of time with my children? Will my daughter have the same cell phone in 20 years? How about those Nintendo games? Will they be around even five years from now? Don't even get me started on DVD's and MP3 Players. I'll have to think a little harder this year about getting them lasting presents not "techno" presents. You don't see a lot of commercials for gifts that last 30 years or more unless you're talking diamond earrings… hint hint Michael.

The best Christmas memory I have has little to do with anything I received and everything to do with how we gave. When I was in about third grade my brother and I collected toys and stuffed animals from all of our classmates at Birch Grove Elementary School. We then dropped these off at the state hospital in Brainerd on our way to Grandmas. The people at the hospital were so excited it made me forget the miserable car ride and my dad's pipe! My daughter has been making handmade items to sell for charity over the past several years. Three years ago she bought a goat at Heifer International, last year she sent a check for $100.00 to Operation Smile and this year she and her cousin raised $165.00 to send to one.org to end world hunger. I am so proud of her and I pray that these acts might be her special Christmas memories also. Merry Christmas and a Happy New Year to you all. My gift to you in addition to some of my holiday favorite recipes is my favorite quote.

They may see the good you do as self serving.
Continue to do good.
They may see your generosity as grandstanding.
Continue to be generous.
They may see your warm and caring nature as a sign of weakness.
Continue to be warm and caring.
For you see, in the end, it is between you and God.
It was never between you and them anyway.
~ Mother Theresa

Grandpa Allard's Oyster Stew

½ cup butter
½ small, onion diced
1 quart half and half cream
2 (12 ounce) containers fresh shucked oysters, undrained
Salt, pepper and Worcestershire Sauce to taste

Melt butter in a stockpot over medium heat. Cook the onions until tender. Add cream and heat until almost boiling; pour the oysters and their liquid into the pot. Season to taste. Stir continuously until oysters until the oysters curl at the ends. When the oysters curl the stew is finished cooking. Serve immediately.

Grandma's Penuche (Sugar Fudge)

2 cups light brown sugar
1 cup white sugar
¾ cup milk
2 Tablespoons corn syrup
2 Tablespoons real butter
1 teaspoon vanilla
1 cup pecan pieces

Mix sugars, milk and corn syrup in a heavy pan. Cook to a boil, stirring constantly. Reduce to medium heat and cover for two minutes. Uncover and cook carefully without stirring to 236 degrees – soft boil on candy thermometer. Place pan in cold water and cool to 110 degrees on candy thermometer. Add butter and vanilla and beat until thick and creamy and candy loses its gloss. Pour into buttered 8 by 8 inch pan. Sprinkle with pecan pieces. Refrigerate and cut into one inch squares.

Friendship Fruit Sauce

This is a pass along fruit compote that was really popular in the 60's. You begin with a starter and then pass it along. My grandma served the fruit sauce warm over vanilla ice cream. Start this early in December then you can split the starter as a Christmas gift for a neighbor. Include the recipe for the fruit sauce.

Fruit Starter

¾ cup canned peaches in heavy syrup, drained and cut into pieces
¾ cup canned pineapple chunks in heavy syrup, drained
6 maraschino cherries cut in half
1 ½ cup sugar
One package Red Star Instant Blend dry yeast

Combine ingredients and place in a glass jar with a loose cover. (An apothecary jar is perfect.) Set in a fairly warm place. Stir several times the first day, then stir once a day for 13 days. At the end of two weeks use one cup to make the fruit sauce and give the rest away.

Fruit Sauce

1 cup fermented fruit
½ cup peaches in heavy syrup, drained and cut into pieces

½ half cup pineapple chunks in heavy syrup, drained
6 maraschino cherries cut in half
1 cup sugar

Combine all ingredients and place back in loose cover jar. Stir daily for one week. Sauce can be served after one week. Heat and serve over ice cream. No need to refrigerate. Sauce will keep for many months if you add sugar and fruit every two weeks.

New Year's Resolutions
(Published 2009)

Here is a riddle for you: What is greater than God, more evil than the Devil, the poor have it, the rich don't need it and if you eat it you will die??? I will tell you the answer at the end of the column if you can't figure it out.

Today I sat down to write my new year's resolutions for 2009 and possibly work them into a column. Yes I resolve to exercise more, drink at least eight glasses of water a day and skip the chocolate. I also vow to try to read a book a week, keep a daily journal and take more bubble baths. I resolve to hug my children more (when they let me) and I will try not to nag them about shutting off the lights once they leave the room. I also resolve to be a mom who is "less embarrassing" to her kids while in public. And last but not least, I think it should be a resolution that Mike and I have a dinner date once a month. There, that should cover it. But does it really?

Then I watched "Last Letters Home" and I cried my eyes out. This is a documentary about families who have lost loved ones as soldiers in Iraq only to receive letters from them delivered after their deaths. I honestly think it as the saddest, purist form of human suffering I have ever witnessed. How do I "resolve" to take more bubble baths after knowing how much others are doing to support our country? We live among mothers, fathers, brothers, sisters, husbands, wives and children of those sacrificing their lives in war and I think I am doing enough? Our community has many families facing terrible financial and personal difficulties, loss of jobs, illness, depression and yes, even hunger. Have I helped in every way I can? What have I done in 2008 to reach out to those in need? Sometimes a smile or a nod of understanding is all it takes to make a difference. Can I do more? Can together WE do more?

The answer to the riddle above is "Nothing". What is greater than God? Nothing. What is more evil than the Devil? Nothing. What do the poor have? Nothing. What do the rich need? Nothing. And if we eat nothing we will surely die. So simple yet it speaks volumes. I would add this to the list: What is the worst thing I can do if I see a stranger, friend or neighbor in need? Nothing.

It is with new eyes I have updated my 2009 resolutions. I will cook too much and bring a meal to a neighbor. I will buy mittens, socks and boots on clearance and drop them at the free store or school. I will give everyone a free smile as I have plenty to share. I will check with the school to see if a child or teen needs lunch money to tide them over for a couple of weeks. I will leave books I have finished at random places so others can enjoy them as well. My list is not yet complete but it's a start. Can it be more simple? I will not stand by and do nothing, I will DO something.

"Do all the good you can. By all the means you can. In all the ways you can. In all the places you can. At all the times you can. To all the people you can. As long as ever you can." ~ John Wesley

Aunt Diane's Hamburger Soup

1 pound hamburger
1 small onion, chopped

Brown the hamburger and onion together with Lawry's seasoning salt and pepper. Drain and place in a 4 quart crock pot. Add the following:

1 quart water
3 cups cubed potatoes
⅓ cup sliced carrots

½ cup sliced celery
1 Tablespoon ketchup
1 (6 ounce) can tomato sauce
2 beef bouillon cubes
1 Tablespoon sugar
½ teaspoon dried basil

Jack's Pepperoni Pizza Casserole

1 cup egg noodles, cooked and drained
½ pound hamburger, browned and drained
1 cup pizza sauce
2 cups mozzarella cheese
About 30 pepperoni slices

In an 8 by 8 glass pan layer noodles, hamburger, pizza sauce, cheese and top with pepperoni. Bake at 350 degrees for 25 minutes.

Baked Spaghetti Tucci Benucci Style

This is a recipe I truly love. After enjoying this dish several times at Tucci Benucci's restaurant at the Mall of America my sister-cousin and I came up with our own version. It's really messy to prepare but the taste is excellent and because you serve it with a variety of pasta sauces it's a great recipe to serve a crowd that might include vegetarian guests.

6 cups Italian Blended Cheese (This can be bought pre-packaged or use a combination of Italian cheeses totaling 6 cups.)
30 ounces ricotta cheese
3 egg yolks
4 cups Alfredo sauce
3 egg whites beaten stiff
8 cups cooked spaghetti noodles rinsed and drained

Preheat oven to 350 degrees. Combine Italian cheese, ricotta cheese and egg yolks. Mix well. Fold the Alfredo sauce with the egg whites. Add the Alfredo mixture to the cheese mixture then add the cooked spaghetti. Toss with your hands. (This is the messy part) Press mixture into a greased 9 by 13 pan. Place the 9 by 13 pan inside a larger jellyroll pan filled with water. Bake for 1 hour. Allow to set up for 10 minutes before cutting into squares like a cake. Serve with your choice of Alfredo, Marinara or a meat sauce. A combination of two sauces makes a beautiful presentation.

Working at Rosie's Café

Finding a winter job in high school was never hard on the North Shore, three words, Lutsen Ski Hill. My brother worked outside making snow and helping park cars, I worked in the lodge cafeteria. With these jobs came free ski passes but when you had to work every Saturday and Sunday it was hard to get in more than one or two ski days a season. There was the assumption that if you worked at the ski hill you were a skier. Wrong. I was a terrible skier. I totally embarrassed a "ski date" by chickening out at the top of the hill. He had to let me put my skis between his like a small child and zig zag all the way to the bottom. (He never called back....hmmmm...I wonder why?)

I did, however, really like ski sweaters and bought several with my employee discount at the ski shop. Now days I think they refer to people as posers if they wear clothes for sports they do not participate in...yes I was a ski poser. My job was fun though. I worked at Rosie's Café before it was "officially" named Rosie's. The real Rosie had been working there since 1967. She is one of those ladies that, if you close your eyes and picture her, it's always with a huge smile on her face. My Aunt Marcia and Rosie's daughter Julie worked at the café in the 70's. She claimed it was her last year then. I teased her about this when I worked there in the 80's. Every season was going to be her last season on the hill.

In the kitchen it was my job to crack the eggs for breakfast and put them in gallon jars. Then I helped bake cinnamon rolls and fill the hot chocolate machine with syrup. I loved dipping Butterfinger bars in hot cocoa for a mid morning snack. It was also my job to take all the trash to the dumpster across the parking lot. I almost killed myself several times a day dodging cars and slipping on the ice. One day I tried to stack all the trash on the deck. By the early afternoon there was a HUGE pile of garbage outside the door and that did not go over well with Rosie. She had me hauling those bags lickety split!

At lunchtime we made piles of French fries and hamburgers. The locals had a table right in from of the café so I could see all my friends who had come out skiing. I had to keep close eyes on the lunch trays at the end of the day as they sometimes disappeared for "sledding" out front. I knew I failed when I had to pick trays out of the snow the following morning.

My husband Mike and I decided to take our kids to Lutsen a few weeks ago on their first big hill ski trip. You'll never guess who answered the 800 number when I called to make a reservation? Yup, Rosie. I asked her is this would be her last season. She just laughed and said "We'll see."

> *"Skiing is the only sport where you spend an arm and*
> *a leg to break an arm and a leg." ~ Unknown*

Breakfast recipes to feed the ENTIRE ski hill!
<u>Scrambled Eggs to Feed 100</u>

17 dozen eggs
16 teaspoons salt
2 pounds butter, melted
20 cups milk (1 gallon plus 1 quart)

Beat eggs add melted butter. Heat milk and salt. Add eggs and butter to milk. Do not stir. Put in 2 large roasters. Bake at 350 degrees for ½ hour, stir. Bake for another ½ hour stir, serve immediately.

Oven Fried Bacon to Feed 100

18 lb sliced bacon

Arrange slices in rows on rimmed baking sheets, across the pan with fat edges slightly overlapping lean edges. Bake 375 degrees without turning 20 to 25 minutes until bacon is slightly crisp. DO NOT OVERCOOK. Skim off excess fat as needed. Drain thoroughly on paper towels. Allows 3 slices per serving.

Buttermilk Pancakes to Feed 100

10 cups flour
10 Tablespoons sugar
10 teaspoons baking powder
5 teaspoons soda
2 ½ teaspoons salt

10 eggs
1 ¼ cups oil
10 cups buttermilk

Mix the dry ingredients together well. Mix the wet ingredients together well. Add the wet ingredients to the dry ingredients and mix until just moist, don't over beat. Laddle batter onto well greased hot griddle. Flip when bubbles rise to the top of batter and edges are lightly brown. Check for doneness. Serve immediately with butter and syrup.

Bread Sacks and Snowmobile Boots

My mom had a drawer full of bread sacks in her kitchen. We never thought of throwing them away. We used them to carry lunches in the woods when we built forts. We used them for cleaning so they wouldn't get the rest of the laundry soiled waiting for wash day. But what I remember the most was putting one on each foot before putting feet into my snowmobile boots. (They kept your feet dry if you don't count the sweating.) And we loved to snowmobile! My parents belonged to a club with several of the neighbors from the West End. We owned two white Polaris sleds that I thought were incredibly fast. On our own, my brother and I rode the high lines behind the house, but with Mom and Dad we rode all over the county.

Dad liked to snowmobile the old logging roads, the 600 Road, the Consolidated Road and the trails from Schroeder to Finland. Gary and I liked to snowmobile the rail road tracks where we could "roll the banks" and ride the bumpy tracks. In Finland we would always stop by the Apollo for pizza. A thin crust special with everything except the anchovies! There was a juke box and a pool table so it seemed like there was lots of music and laughing before the cold, cold ride home.

On one particular outing the whole club decided to have a cookout on the shore of Crescent Lake. We rode across the lake to what seemed to be a good spot, just out of the wind so we could build a campfire. We roasted hot dogs and marshmallows. Let me tell you nothing tastes better than a hot dog toasted over a campfire and a cup of hot chocolate. It was a picture perfect, until we put the fire out. As we stamped down the snow to put out the coals, garbage and old diapers started flying up. It turns out of all the places on shore to build a campfire we had chosen one right over someone's garbage dump! Yuck!

Sometimes the trip home would be bitter cold and our feet would freeze inside our bread sacks and boots. Our fingers inside our knitted mittens were even colder. It was all you could do to hang on to Dad for dear life and hope to be home soon. I like to sing songs to myself as no one could hear my terrible voice out in the wild over the roar of the snowmobile. When we got home we would hang our mittens on clothespins and hangers behind the woodstove. The steam would roll off of them as the ice began to melt and there was that special smell of wet wool as it dries that you never forget.

I cherish these childhood memories more than anything, cold and all. You might want to hang on to a couple of bread sacks the next time you need a liner for your boots, just remember to turn them inside out to keep the crumbs off your socks!

"If you obey all the rules, you miss all the fun!" ~ Katharine Hepburn

Marshmallow Hot Cocoa

8 teaspoons sugar
4 teaspoons baking cocoa
4 cups milk
1 ½ cups miniature marshmallows
1 teaspoon vanilla

In a saucepan, combine the first four ingredients. Cook and stir over medium heat until the marshmallows are melted, about 8 minutes. Remove from the heat; stir in vanilla. Ladle into mugs or into a thermos and take along to the campfire.

Chocolate Peanut Butter S'mores

Graham Crackers
Marshmallows
Peanut Butter Cups

Easy peasy..... Just replace the usual chocolate bar with peanut butter cup and you have a whole new taste. But remember to remove the peanut butter cup paper wrapper before you smoosh it between the graham crackers and toasted marshmallow. The paper is hard to see around the campfire but it tastes yucky!

Honey Butter Campfire Biscuits

1 can biscuits
8 Tablespoons butter
¼ cup honey

Whip honey and butter together and place in a squeeze bottle. Roll out a biscuit with your hands so that it becomes elongated and about one inch thick at the center. Wrap it tightly around the end of your campfire stick and pinching it as you go to ensure that it stays on the stick while cooking. When done wrapping, the biscuit should take up about six inches of the stick. Heat over the campfire until golden brown. Pull it off the stick, pour butter down the hole left by the stick, and enjoy. Messy but delicious!!

What the Devil Does That Mean?

I have been known to be a little gullible in my day. (OK maybe a lot.) It might be from my sheltered "Up North" childhood or maybe I just like to buy into a good story. Sometimes the bigger the whopper the better. Its fun and I have traded a few myself. My husband Mike on the other hand is very skeptical. He likes solid proof and hard evidence. I will come home all excited about a story and he'll roll his eyes and say "Right Sandy, how big was the hook they used on that one?" This got me thinking about stories we accept as fact but when examined maybe started out with a small grain of truth and a whole lot of fiction was added just to jazz it up. I heard a really good one yesterday.

I was in Buffalo having my son's snowboard fixed. I happened to mention we were planning a family trip to Lutsen. The owner was a huge fan of the North Shore and a history buff. He likes to celebrate the Fisherman's Picnic atop the old bank building in Grand Marais. We traded a few stories back and forth, and then he asked me if I knew how Devil's Track Lake came by its name. "Is it in the shape of a cloven hoof?" I asked. Nope. "Does it have something to do with cake?" (Devils Food…..) Nada. "Was there a Tasmanian Devil on the loose in the North Woods at one time or another?" Yeah right. Ok, now I was curious.

Here is the lore: The Indians noticed strange and unusual tracks circling the lake. These tracks could not be identified as the tracks of wolves, deer or fox. In fact, nothing in the forest was known to make such markings, so they decided they could only be "tracks of the Devil himself". Thus naming the lake Devil's Track Lake. What really made these strange and unusual tracks?? According to my storyteller from Buffalo the tracks were actually made by an old trapper with a snowshoe and a peg leg!! I laughed out loud and asked what he'd been drinking! He argued that it was true and then I argued that an old trapper would also have fastened a snowshoe to his peg leg and no one would have been the wiser. Good point, he conceded but he still felt the story was based on fact not fiction. As it turned out he was partly right. I made a couple of calls to the historical society of Cook County and did some internet research. The most I could come up with was there might have been a man living in the area who lost his leg in a war. The lake though, was named after an Ojibwa word meaning negative feeling or spirits. You let me know if you have the "real story" or another bar version that can make me laugh. Who knows how they came up with the name for "Castle Danger" anyway? I've always been curious about that.

Sven walked into a bar in Grand Marais and asked the bartender if he's heard the latest Cook County High School joke? "I'm warning you" said the barman "I'm a CCHS graduate". "Dat's alright" said Sven "Then I'll tell it real sloooooowly."

Chicken Deviled Eggs

6 hardboiled eggs
½ cup cooked chicken, minced (measure before mincing)
¼ cup mayonnaise
2 Tablespoons minced sweet onion
1 Tablespoon sweet pickle relish
1 Tablespoon minced parsley
2 teaspoons small capers, drained and finely chopped
1 teaspoon Dijon mustard
½ teaspoon dry mustard powder
¼ teaspoon salt
Dash of hot pepper sauce, or to taste
Paprika, for garnish

Cut hardboiled eggs lengthwise in half. Place yolks in a bowl and mash with a fork until crumbled. Add minced chicken, mayonnaise, sweet onion, sweet pickle relish, parsley, capers, Dijon mustard, mustard powder, salt, and hot pepper salt. Mix until evenly combined.

Fill egg whites with mounds of egg yolk mixture, mounding some over the white part as well as the yolk hole so each bite gets some of the filling. Sprinkle deviled eggs lightly with paprika. Decorate with slivers of olives, roasted red peppers, and tomatoes, along with fresh herb sprigs such as chives, baby basil leaves, dill, or parsley, if desired.

Cover and refrigerate until ready to serve. Best made a day in advance to let flavors meld.

Sweet Deviled Carrots

½ pound carrots cut into 2 inch sticks
⅛ teaspoon salt
1 Tablespoon butter
¼ cup brown sugar
1 Tablespoon prepared mustard
¼ cup chopped parsley

Cook carrots with salt in boiling water to cover until tender. Drain. Place butter, sugar and mustard in a large saucepan. Cook over low heat, stirring, until syrupy, about 3 minutes. Add cooked carrots and toss gently to coat with sauce. Add salt, if needed. Place in a heated serving dish. Sprinkle with parsley. Yield: 2 servings

Cinnamon Devils Food Cupcakes

2 ⅔ cups all-purpose flour
1 ½ cups unsweetened cocoa powder
1 Tablespoon cinnamon
2 teaspoons baking powder
1 ½ teaspoons salt
1 teaspoon baking soda
3 ½ cups sugar
1 ¼ cups freshly brewed coffee, cooled to room temperature
1 ¼ cups buttermilk
¾ cup oil
2 large eggs
2 large egg yolks
1 teaspoon vanilla
1 ½ cups miniature semisweet chocolate chips

Preheat oven to 325 degrees. Prepare regular muffin tins and line with paper liners. In a bowl sift together flour, cocoa, cinnamon, baking powder, baking soda and salt. In a extra large bowl combine sugar, coffee, buttermilk, oil, eggs, egg yolks and vanilla; beat well with an electric mixer until thoroughly combined. Add in the dry ingredients; beat on medium speed until blended, scraping bowl occasionally. Stir in the mini chocolate chips. Spoon the batter evenly between the prepared muffin tins. Bake for about 20 to 25 minutes, or until puffed and the center is just firm to the touch. Transfer the cupcakes to racks and cool completely before frosting. Makes 40 cupcakes. Frost with cream cheese frosting.

My Aunties

Aunt Donna, Aunt Marcia and Aunt Debbie
holding baby Sandy, Easter 1964

My mother came to visit last weekend and with her she brought a picture of me and my Aunties. These were three of her younger sisters, my Aunt Donna, Aunt Marcia and Aunt Debbie. I think I am about five months old and the girls had each just received a new pair of pajamas for Easter so my mom took a picture. I looked surprised and maybe a little scared but I also think I look a lot like them in some ways. When I was older my mom would cut my hair in a similar fashion. She would put pink beauty shop tape across my bangs then try to cut them in a straight line. Sometimes I would wiggle so they didn't always come out straight, even with the tape.

Growing up my grandparents lived less than a mile from our house so I spent a lot of time with my aunts when I was little. They introduced me to Band Stand. I liked the part where Dick Clark would play a new song then the dancers would rate the song and say "It had a good beat Dick but I couldn't dance to it." Whatever that meant. My Aunt Marcia would walk around the house with white Noxzema all over her face and I would beg her to put some on me but then I wouldn't like the tingling and make her take it off. This is also the aunt that threatened to cut off my tongue with Grandma's giant pinking shears if I stuck it out at her again. (This only encouraged me to do it more.)

My Aunt Donna was a trickster. She would color in my coloring books then sign her name at the bottom of the picture like a real artist would do. She was very good at coloring so I would ask her to write my name next to her picture so my mom would think I colored it. She said she wrote Sandy Marie but actually she had written Donna Marie in cursive so I couldn't read it. My mom then knew I was fibbing when I tried to pass it off as mine. Aunt Donna also took me on a sled ride down the driveway once and then she jumped off. I almost lost my two front teeth when I hit the front of the neighbor's car. The teeth turned real black and hurt, but eventually they went back to normal. I sure was suspicious of Aunt Donna after that!

My Aunt Debbie was shy and quiet as I remember her. She would babysit my brother and me sometimes. I don't recall her ever threatening to cut off my tongue or cause me bodily harm. I know I was lucky to have these three taking care of me and teaching me how to be a girl. I loved the clothes they wore and I watched how they put on their makeup. They grew their hair long and straight down their backs. Sometimes they would lay their hair on the ironing board and press it flat before going out on a date. Other times they rolled their hair in orange juice cans and bobby pins for long, loose curls.

I put the framed picture of me and my aunties on my desk and it reminds me of their smiles, their laughter and that they loved and cared about me. I treasure these gifts.

"Every so often, I like to go to the window, look up, and smile for a satellite picture."
~ Stephen Wright

Chocolate Wet Cake

2 cups flour
2 cups sugar

Mix well and set aside/

1 ½ cups butter
4 Tablespoons cocoa
1 cup water

Mix in a saucepan. Bring this to a boil. Combine with the flour and sugar mix. Add
½ cup sour milk
1 teaspoon baking soda,
1 teaspoon cinnamon
1 teaspoon vanilla
2 eggs

Mix well. Pour into a 9 by 13 pan. Bake at 375 degrees for 25 minutes or until done. Frost as desired.

* To sour milk I add one teaspoon vinegar or lemon juice to regular milk and let it sit for one minute.

Aunties Corn Bread - Bonnie Moe

2 cups Bisquick
1 cup sugar
2 heaping Tablespoons cornmeal
1 cup milk
2 eggs
1 ½ sticks softened butter

Stir ingredients together and place in greased 9 by 9 inch pan. Bake at 350 degrees 25 to 30 minutes.

Gelatin Magic Milkshakes

1 cup milk
1 (4 serving size) package of gelatin (peach and lemon are my favorites!)
1 pint vanilla ice cream

Put milk and gelatin in blender and blend for 30 seconds. Add softened vanilla ice cream. Blend an additional 1 minute. Enjoy!

Easter Bonnets and Silly Faces

Our Easters were not usually spent on the North Shore for obvious reasons as bunnies don't like to hide their eggs in a foot of snow. We usually went to visit my mom's older sister Bonnie in Rochester. These were fun trips because my grandparents lived there too and we could see my mom's younger siblings. My mother had four younger sisters and one younger brother. Her youngest sister, Donna was nine when I was born. She was a rowdy girl that got away with things my mom said she'd never dared try. We thought she was cool and lippy. She called us younger kids "pinheads", I still don't know if that is a good thing or a bad thing. She is also the aunt that let me watch "The Twilight Zone" T.V. show long before I should have. I was deathly afraid of sleeping upstairs for years after seeing one particular episode. My mom was not too happy about it as upstairs was the only place to sleep at Grandma's house.

Decorating for Easter was fun. My Aunt Bonnie taught us how to clean out real eggs by poking a pin hole into each end and then blowing real hard on one end until the egg white and egg yolk came out the other end. Then we would dye the eggs and hang them on branches to make Egg Trees. Once the eggs dried they became brittle and broke so you had to make a new tree every year. I liked to dye the boiled eggs. The smell of vinegar, as it was used to set the colors, brings back this memory every time. After Easter we would make the boiled eggs into yummy egg salad.

My cousins lived on a farm so there were lots of places to hide Easter eggs for a hunt. In the morning you'd first have to find your basket then you could use this to collect the treat filled eggs. We never got baby chickens or bunnies in our baskets but there were usually plenty running around the yard. Each year my cousin Dawn and I would get a pair of little white gloves and a bonnet from the Easter Bunny.

When my children were small, we hosted a backyard Easter egg hunt at our house. Every child who came brought a dozen treat filled eggs and we dumped them all together in a wagon, then while the children played a game, the dads hid all the eggs. Each child could then find twelve eggs to take home. Usually they did not find their own so each egg was a surprise. I also bought two 25 piece puzzles and 50 white plastic eggs. On one puzzle I put a sticker of a lady bug on the back of each puzzle piece and on the other puzzle I put a sticker of a star on the back of each puzzle piece. Then we put the pieces into the eggs with matching stickers on the eggs and hid them. The kids formed two teams the "ladybugs" and the "stars". Then they went hunting for eggs and the first team to find all their puzzle pieces and put the puzzle together won a prize. This game really got them running, the parents had a blast just watching them get so excited.

Of course any holiday means picture time. My mom would try her best to take pictures of everyone during the Easter visit then send the film in a mailer to Duluth when we got home. I remember one particular Easter when I was about thirteen the film came back and I was in BIG TROUBLE! There was a picture of a girl sticking out her tongue at the camera and making a face! I was told that this was very rude and how I had ruined the picture. I felt bad until I looked more closely at the photo. "Mom, that's not me, that's your sister Donna!" Whoops! Thanks Aunt Donna, now who's the pinhead?

> *"Easter says you can put truth in a grave, but it won't stay there".* ~*Clarence W. Hall*

Sandy Holthaus

Peek-a-Boo Eggs

12 slices Canadian bacon (or ham)
12 slices Swiss cheese
12 eggs
½ pint cream
Grated parmesan cheese (optional)

Line shallow pan with Canadian bacon, add layer of cheese. Break eggs over all. Drizzle cream over until the yolks peek through. Bake at 450 degrees for 10 minutes. Remove and sprinkle with grated Parmesan cheese. Return to oven and bake 8 to 10 minutes longer. Cut in squares and serve. Serves: 6 to 9

Eggstremely Easy Eggs (This is a good recipe to use with the blown out eggs from your egg tree.)

12 eggs
1 pound bacon
1 (8 ounce) carton sour cream
1 cup shredded cheddar cheese

Dice and fry the bacon. Drain on paper towels. Scramble the eggs with a little milk. Place a layer of eggs in the bottom of a casserole dish. Carefully spread the sour cream on the eggs. Sprinkle fried bacon over the sour cream. Top with cheese. Bake in a 350 degree oven for 25 to 30 minutes. This dish can be made the night before and baked in the morning. Serves: 6. Quick and delicious!

Breakfast Calzone

1 loaf of frozen bread dough
4 large eggs
¼ pound cubed ham
¼ pound sliced, cubed cheese (cheddar, American, or Swiss)

¼ pound diced pepper (optional)
Salt and pepper to taste

Scramble eggs - do not fully cook. Cool eggs. Roll out bread dough to about 14 to 16 inches in diameter. Spread eggs over dough, put the ham over eggs, and cheese over the ham, and peppers over the cheese. Roll jelly roll fashion. Place on a greased cookie sheet. Grease calzone lightly. Bake at 375 degrees for 35 to 45 minutes. Slice about 1 inch wide and serve while hot.

A Wedding in God's Country

My niece just called and asked if I would cut and serve the cake at her wedding in 7 months. She is good with the details and isn't leaving anything to chance. She has booked all our hair appointments too. I was thinking about what I was doing seven months before my wedding...oh yes, I was dating! Although Mike and I dated for four years, our engagement was a relatively short, only three months. My dream wedding was to be married lakeside in Grand Marais on the lawn of Naniboujou. This is a beautiful resort east of town with fabulous food and Cree Indian Designs painted on the ceilings. As it turned out I was married on the first day of spring in Calmar, Iowa. (What girl dreams of a wedding in Calmar?) We were married at The Calmar Guest House with 30 relatives. We wanted to keep the ceremony small and intimate as Zoë was only four at the time and we thought a big church service would be overwhelming. The priest was soo wonderful. He blessed wedding rings not only for Mike and me but also a little one for Zoë. I don't think there was a dry eye in the house as Mike slipped a ring on each of our fingers. My mother read from Kahlil Gibran. Months later we received a video tape of four of Mike's friends trying to crash the ceremony. One even climbed a big tree on the front lawn to peek in the windows. It was hilarious! We had no idea there was such a ruckus going on right outside the front door of the guest house.

After our wedding Mike and I looked forward to the reception where we could relax and celebrate with our family, friends and co-workers. Yes, many of them drove all the way to Decorah, Iowa just to be with us. My friends couldn't believe we would get married in Iowa! (Here's a kicker, Mike's parents honeymooned in Grand Marais! *True story!*)

When I first met Mike he claimed to be from God's country and I said this was impossible for two reasons. One: Everyone in Minnesota knows that Cook County is the only true God's Country, and Two: He was talking about Iowa! The only thing I knew about Iowa was that it had flat land, corn and it was the butt of some really bad jokes, usually involving pigs. I will now admit that I was wrong. Iowa has a God's country too, Decorah. Beautiful bluffs, rivers and rolling hills.

I found my engagement ring sitting in the snow on a bluff overlooking Mike's childhood home. (He was lucky a bald eagle didn't steal it before he popped the question.) I was truly shocked and overwhelmed. It was very romantic.

Time really does fly by faster the older you get. It is hard to believe that we have been married since March 21, 1998. March 21st is also my mother in laws birthday. If Mike forgets this day he knows he'll be in trouble with someone. This year we will celebrate together with Mike's parents on a ski trip to Lutsen and maybe lunch at Nanaboujou Lodge. It doesn't get any better than an anniversary celebration in God's country.

Excellent marriage advice: Just like two and two always adds up to four, kindness and forgiveness is ALWAYS right, hate and revenge is ALWAYS wrong. It's a fool proof system. Just stick to this one simple rule and you couldn't make a mistake if you tried.

Here are three must have recipes for the first year of marriage to keep it sweet!

Almond Joy Bars

2 cups graham cracker crumbs
¼ cup powdered sugar
½ cup butter
1 can Sweetened Condensed milk
1 ½ cups coconut

1 cup chocolate chips

½ cup slivered almonds

Mix crumbs, sugar, and butter. Press in 9 by 9 pan and bake 10 minutes in 300 degree oven. Mix milk and coconut, spread over crumbs and put back in oven 10 more minutes. Put chocolate chips on top then sprinkle with almonds. Let cool. Cut into squares.

Caramel Apple Crisp

Apple Filling:
5 large Granny Smith apples - peeled, cored, and thinly sliced

½ cup sugar

1 Tablespoon all-purpose flour

½ teaspoon ground cinnamon

1 Tablespoon lemon juice

¼ cup water

Crumble:
1 ½ cups all-purpose flour

1 cup brown sugar

1 cup quick cooking oats

1 cup butter, softened

Caramel Sauce:
1 (14 ounce) package individually wrapped caramels, unwrapped

1 (5 ounce) can evaporated milk

Preheat oven to 350 degrees. In a medium size bowl, toss apples with sugar, flour, cinnamon, lemon juice, and water; spread evenly into a 8 by 8 pan. In another bowl, mix together flour, brown sugar, oats, and butter; spoon mixture evenly over apples. In a heavy sauce pan over low heat, melt the caramels with the evaporated milk. Heat, stirring frequently, until mixture has a smooth consistency. Drizzle the caramel sauce over the top of the crumble. Bake in preheated oven for about 45 minutes (apple mixture will bubble and topping will be golden brown).

Bananas Foster: Don't be afraid to keep the home fires burning!

⅓ cup butter
⅓ cup brown sugar
Three ripe bananas (not too ripe)
¼ teaspoon cinnamon
2 Tablespoons crème de cocoa or banana liqueur
¼ cup rum

In large skillet melt butter, add brown sugar and stir until melted. Add bananas and cook gently over medium heat for about two minutes. Sprinkle with cinnamon. Stir in liqueur. Gently toss to coat bananas. Remove from heat and in a well ventilated area pour rum over mixture and ignite with a long match. Flame will die out quickly. Serve over vanilla ice cream.

Lovin' Summer

It's almost here and I cannot wait! Summer means sleeping late, relaxing by the lake, and then after about a week hearing the kids say...."We're bored"! There is "Nothing to do". My children did not invent this mentality as I know for a fact we drove our mom crazy with these words day after day until she told us to go outside or she'd give us housework. I personally have nothing against child labor but then again it is fun to do some things in the summer that you would never do any other time of year. And because I write a cooking column of course all my ideas surround food of some kind. As you will see below not all foods are meant for consumption, like zucchini (Yuck!), but for the most part these recipes are easy and delicious. I call them "50 Ways to Leave Your Boredom". (Paul Simon fans will get this joke.)

1. Food Fight Party – Adventurous moms will allow this party once and maybe only once but it is fun. From experience I suggest the following rules: Rule one: If you won't eat it don't throw it! This prevents the neighborhood children from making disgusting concoctions of refrigerator left over's and throwing them on my head. (Try to get old cottage cheese and gravy out of your hair...not easy!) Good ideas for ammo: Chocolate pudding, Hershey's syrup, whipping cream in a can, Jello, cake, ice cream, you get the idea. Rule Two: To play you must be inside the circle. We used a garden hose to make the boundaries, that way if you needed a break you had a safe place to go. Just step outside the circle. Rule Three: No food can be thrown from outside the circle. Rule Four: Don't throw food at the cameraman. And Rule Five: Outside game only!
2. Powder Sugar Fishing – Take powdered sugar doughnuts and

tie them to a string. Attach the string to a pole and dangle the doughnut over someone lying on their back. The "fish" try to bite the doughnut. We use powdered sugar because they are the messiest.

3. Blue Food Breakfast – Make everything blue using food coloring. Blue pancakes, blue scrambled eggs and blue milk. This comes from Zoë's favorite book "No Blue Food." I think the milk is the hardest to get past the color. It just doesn't seem right.

4. Make a Candy Gram – Using candy bars and treats to make words on a poster board are really fun. The kids learn to be creative too. The RIESEN for this greeting is to wish you a CAREFREE summer. Don't go NUTS while you are fighting the MOUNDS of people at the park. Don't worry about getting CHUNKY as there will be GOOD and PLENTY of time to worry about that next winter! HUGS AND KISSES! Your, SWEEHEART.

5. Whip Cream Cars – A can of whipping cream and matchbox cars are a fun afternoon game. Cover an outdoor picnic table with whipping cream and drive the cars through the "snow." It will be good practice for Winter driving.

6. Jello Shots – (Settle down, not those kind of Jello shots, this is for the kids.) Try making your favorite flavor combinations of Jello and juice. Just replace the cold water with fruit juice and put the Jello into little cups. My favorite is peach Jello with orange juice. (I don't know where I came up with this combination but is to die for.)

7. Gold Fish Trail – This is like Hansel and Gretel following bread crumbs into the forest but I think the orange gold fish crackers show up better. Have one child start the trail and see if the rest can follow it. You might want to take the family dog along to pick up the crackers along the way.

8. Sweet Bubbles – Make homemade bubbles and use flyswatters over the outside air conditioning unit when it runs and you will not believe the bubbles! Use two flyswatters as one is

just not enough. Sweet Bubbles: 1 Tablespoon Corn Syrup, 2 Tablespoons dish soap and one cup water, mix well.

9. Pick Apples and Make Apple Sauce – There is nothing like homemade apple sauce and the kids will actually know that it doesn't have to come from a jar. Peel, core and slice six cups of apples, (try different varieties) place in a pan and add two cups of water, cook down to make sauce add more water if needed, mash with potato masher and add sugar to taste.

10. Make Celery Roses – If you cut a stalk of celery about two inches from the bottom you will see the part usually thrown out is a perfect rose. Dip in paint and press on paper. Pretty!

11. Peanut Butter Play Dough - 1 cup smooth peanut butter, ½ cup light corn syrup, ½ Tablespoon vanilla extract and 1 ¼ cups powdered sugar. Mix peanut butter, corn syrup and vanilla together. Gradually add powdered sugar. Store covered at room temperature.

12. Oreo Salad – We all have pot lucks in the summer and this is the most kid friendly to make. Better yet let them make it. Put about 15 Oreo's in a Ziploc bag. Smash into small pieces. Mix with a large container of cool whip and serve. Whole Oreos on top look good but wait until just before serving as they get mushy if they sit too long.

13. Cooked Spaghetti Art – Cook spaghetti and dye with food coloring. Using scissors cut the spaghetti into various sizes to make lines and pictures on the paper. The spaghetti will stick once it is dry.

14. Volunteer for Meals on Wheels – Kids and parents can help deliver food to the community in the summer. Contact senior dining for more information. This is fun and only takes about an hour out of your day to help those in need.

15. Crumby Car Clean Up – Hand out the vacuum and those little food droppings will disappear like magic from mom's car. (The family dog in the car for 15 minutes can have the same effect. Whichever works for you.)

16. Stone Soup – Invite all the neighbors to bring vegetables over

and make stone soup. You provide a huge pot full of water and place a clean stone at the bottom. Peeling, chopping and dicing veggies can be lots of fun when you do it together. In the end you have a wonderful tasty soup.

17. Ants on a Log – Using the leftover celery from idea number 10, cut into sticks and add peanut butter and raisins. If you don't like raisins use M&Ms, the ants are bigger and they taste better too.

18. Pick Strawberries at the local patch – These are soo good you'll just want to wash them and eat them the minute you get home. Try to save a few for project ideas below.

19. Coffee Can Ice Cream – Using both a 12 ounce and a 39 ounce coffee can you have an ice cream maker ready to go. In the smaller can add one cup of whole milk, one cup of heavy cream, ½ cup of sugar and ½ teaspoon vanilla. Put the cover on the can and tape it to hold in place. Place smaller can into larger can then fill with crushed ice and rock salt. Tape the large cover in place then roll down the hill for 20 or 30 minutes. Eat immediately because you are hot from all that rolling.

20. Tic Tac Toe – Use cereal and raisins for x's and o's. Winner eats the game pieces. Cat games (where you both win) eat their own.

21. Bread Dough Doughnut Holes – Using refrigerator biscuits cut into fours, fry dough in oil then roll in sugar and cinnamon.

22. Make Go Go Juice – Use one cup orange juice concentrate, one cup sliced bananas and one cup pineapple juice. Blend well and drink. This will get you hula hooping in no time!

23. Make Chocolate Clay – Materials: 10 ounces of chocolate (chopped chunks or chips) and one third cup light corn syrup. 1.) Melt the chocolate in a microwave for one minute. Stir. If chocolate is not completely melted, return to the microwave for 30 seconds at a time and stir until smooth. If you don't have a microwave, place the chocolate in the top of a double boiler over hot water and stir until melted. 2.) When the chocolate

is melted, add the corn syrup and blend. 3.) Pour the mixture onto a waxed paper sheet. 4.) Spread the chocolate with your fingers until it's about one half inch thick. 5.) Cover loosely with waxed paper and let it stiffen for at least a couple hours or overnight. The chocolate will become very pliable.

24. Volunteer for Fare For All – This is a great way to teach children about how a food coop works in our community. One Saturday a month throughout the summer. Kid and parent volunteers are welcome!

25. Pop "Real" Popcorn – Buy the kernels and pop them up in a pan. This shows the kids' popcorn doesn't always come out of a microwavable bag. (Don't feel bad, my kids just saw this a month ago.) The smell is awesome!

26. Pudding Paint with Sprinkles – Nuff said!

27. Corn Starch Sidewalk Paint – Mix corn starch, water and tempera paints. I use a muffin pan to make lots of colors. Use brushes to paint on the sidewalks and cement. When it dries the colors are brilliant.

28. Visit the Farmers Market – Lots of locally grown, locally made products. You might even find some veggies for your Stone Soup. (See # 16)

29. Make Apple Cheese Pizza – Use one loaf of frozen bread dough thawed, roll onto pizza pan, top with one cup shredded cheddar cheese, two cups sliced apples, and a mixture of one half teaspoon cinnamon, two Tablespoons flour and one half cup brown sugar. Top with two Tablespoons of butter. Bake in preheated oven at 350 degrees for 20 to 25 minutes.

30. Make Frozen Fruit Cups – Blend berries and bananas in blender. Spoon into Dixie cups and put a Popsicle stick in the center of each cup. Freeze. Remove paper and enjoy.

31. Apple Bobs – Tie strings to apples and hang them in a row on the clothes line at mouth height, with hands behind your back you must eat the entire apple. First one done, wins an apple.

32. Make Dinosaur Food – One fourth cup dirt (Cocoa), one half cup swamp water (milk), two cups crushed bones (sugar),

one half cup fat (softened butter), two and a half cups grass (uncooked quick oats), one half cup squashed bugs (crunchy peanut butter) and one teaspoon muddy water (vanilla). Mix first four ingredients in a saucepan and bring to a boil for one minute. Remove from heat and add grass, bugs and muddy water (oats, peanut butter and vanilla). Drop by Tablespoon onto wax paper, wait for the ice age (let cool) and serve to the cave men.

33. Pass the orange please – Oranges are passed back and forth under their chins between teams of two six times, then the team peels and eats the orange. The first team done wins an orange.

34. Banana Logs – Peel and cut bananas in half. Insert a stick into the end, dip in glass of Hershey's syrup and roll in rice krispies. Yum!

35. Pick Raspberries – Visit a local raspberry grower and pick the reddest, juiciest berries. Then buy some lemon sherbet on the way home. This combination of berries and lemon is unbelievably good.

36. Have a Picnic – Pack a picnic and head out to your favorite park. Don't go to the same park you usually frequent, try a different location and discover new trails. Sandwiches taste better in the great outdoors.

37. Make Monkey Bread – 5 pkgs. Pillsbury refrigerator rolls, one cup sugar, three tbsp. cinnamon, one stick butter, one half cup brown sugar. Cut each roll in quarters and mix sugar and cinnamon together. Toss cut rolls into sugar and cinnamon mixture. Layer in fully greased Bundt pan. Melt butter and add brown sugar. Pour over entire cut and layered pieces. Bake for 35 to 45 minutes at 350 degrees. Turn over onto dish, and serve warm.

38. Potato Stamps – Using large baking potatoes, cut in half then draw a design on the bottom of the potato, carefully cut around the design then cut away the potato from the edge

leaving the design raised on the end of the potato. This then makes a great stamper with any kind of paint.

39. Dirt Cake – Using a clean sand pail and shovel this makes a great beach cake. You will need 12 ounces of gummy worms, one box of Oreo cookie crumbs and two large boxes of instant vanilla pudding (prepared with milk). Mix prepared pudding with 8 ounces of cream cheese, one cup powdered sugar and one stick of softened butter. Fold in 16 ounces of cool whip. Layer in pail pudding, crumbs and worms until you get to the top. Then hang remaining worms over the edge and top with dirt. (Oreo crumbs) Serve with shovel.

40. ABC Bread – Using thawed frozen bread dough make shapes, letters and names on a greased cookie sheet. Brush with egg white and sprinkle with salt or sesame seeds. Bake at 350 degrees until brown.

41. Carrot Catcher – Drop baby carrots into a mason jar while standing with your hand at least 24 inches from the top of the jar. Person with the most carrots in the jar wins the carrots.

42. Fruit Kabobs – Using skewers make kabobs with all kinds of fruit like bananas, oranges and strawberries. The best fruit dip is made with 7 ounces of marshmallow cream mixed with 8 ounces of cream cheese.

43. Graham Cracker Cookies – Honey or Chocolate graham crackers with homemade frosting are delicious. Mix one cup powder sugar with one Tablespoon milk and one half teaspoon vanilla to make the frosting.

44. Pizza Bubble Bread – Sprinkle a pizza pan with corn meal. Seperate one package of refrigerator biscuits and cut each biscuit into four pieces. Mix with ½ cup pizza sauce. Arrange in an eight inch circle on the pan. Top with 1 cup shredded mozzarella cheese. Bake at 400 degrees for 15 minutes.

45. Hot Dog Mummies with Cheese – Slice hot dogs the long way but not all the way through put one fourth of a slice of American cheese into each cut. Then roll a refrigerator biscuit into a long snake, wrap the hot dog like a mummy and place

on a cookie sheet. Bake at 350 degrees for about 8 minutes or until golden brown.

46. Apple Schmear – This is played with tennis rackets and old apples. The pitcher tosses the apple to the batter, who using the tennis racket schmears the apple everywhere. Hint to pitcher: Wear old clothes.

47. Make Octopus Spaghetti – Cook spaghetti noodles and use blue food coloring to make the "water". Cut hot dogs three quarters of the way into eight legs, leaving one quarter not cut at all. (This is the head of the octopus.) Boil hot dogs about three minutes and serve on top of the water.

48. Make Apple Smiles – Using two red apple slices, top one with peanut butter and two mini marshmallows, top the second with peanut butter then put the two together like lips to make an apple smile. Very cute and delicious too.

49. Baby Food Tasting Contest – Buy several jars of baby food and remove the labels after you have numbered and recorded each jar. Have your friends try to identify the baby food flavor first by sight then by smell and finally by taste. The winner gets baby food?

50. And finally – Zucchini Boats – This of course if the ONLY good thing you can do with a zucchini. Carve the center from the biggest zucchini you can find. Don't buy a zucchini just grab one from the post office where the zucchini growers dump them once they have run out of neighbors and friends to give them to. Feel free to add a mast or decorations. You may even wish to christen your boat with a name. Then send it off down a river, stream or lake. Smile as it disappears like the summer will all too soon!

Thanks to my sister-cousin for all her help with these ideas. She is very clever. (I love you Dawn)

How to Hire a Hit Man

If you've heard the rumor, yes it's true - I tried to hire a hit man. I offered him $100.00 cold hard cash…seriously I was at my wits end. Let me explain; the "hit man" was not actually a hired killer he was my Schwann's man and it wasn't a person I was trying to have "taken care of" it was a Chihuahua. You have to ask yourself, what could drive a mild mannered cooking columnist to sink to such a low? (After all the Chihuahua Skippy John Jones is one of my favorite book characters – "Oochiwawa I'm a Chihuahua!" It's just fun to say.) Let me sum it up for you with one letter – P. To phrase it more clearly, as my Grandma used to say, this dog is a "piddle pot."

The day started out innocently enough with a scheduled spring carpet cleaning. As the cleaner set up his equipment I was moving knick knacks and tables. He then asked me to step into a darkened room where, with his carpet cleaning high technology, he showed me bright blue dots covering the ENTIRE ROOM. (If it was luminal we would have had a bloody crime scene.) I was in shock! By the size of these dots it had to be the Chihuahua! (Unless of course the black lab was trying to frame the little dog by leaving teaspoon size trails around the house but I don't think our Labrador watches CSI.) Mr. Carpet Cleaner then proceeded to tell me the cost to remove all these little *"offenses."* My friend let me tell you, I could have had a brand new flat screen TV. But what choice did I have? I had to pay the man and fume at the dog.

The ice cream man just came along at the wrong time. He said he was always worried he was going to hit a dog accidently one day on his route. Then the idea hit me like a brick. I offered him a hundred bucks to our Chihuahua over with the ice cream truck. Cash on the spot no questions asked. He hesitated and laughed nervously but I stared him dead in the eye. I even offered to tie her leash to an old tire to slow her down for him. He of course, being the gentleman that he is, declined my offer, handed me my fudgesicles and left, leaving me to look into the face of the offender with no options but to strangle her myself. Relax, I didn't do it.

Now of course, I am of a more reasonable mind have decided a little (or a lot) of retraining is all she needs. Of course she will not be allowed on our fresh clean carpets EVER AGAIN, but she is still a sweetheart or as Skippy John Jones would say "Ochiwawa it's hard to love a Chihuahua!" I have also decided I am going to focus of the sweeter things in life that start with the letter "P" like Pecan Drops, Peach Pie and Pear Crisp. I might gain five pounds, but the little dog lives.

"If you think dogs can't count, try putting three dog biscuits in your pocket and then giving Fido only two of them". ~Phil Pastoret

Mudge's Pecan Drops - Kim Skildum-Reid

This recipe is easy-peasy and always a big hit.

1 cup brown sugar
2 to 3 Tablespoons water
Pinch of salt
1 egg white
2 to 3 cups Pecan Halves (Grandma says 2, I always go 3)

Preheat oven to 250 degrees. Melt brown sugar, salt, and water over very low heat until it is syrupy. It's okay if it's still a bit grainy. I start with 2 Tablespoons of water, but often add another if it looks a bit too stiff. While melting, beat egg white until semi-stiff peaks. Grandma said soft peaks, but I always go a bit stiffer, so the mixture just stands up in points without flopping over when you take the beaters out. Pour the hot sugar mixture into the egg white while beating. If you can't manage that, pour it in about thirds and beat in between. That keeps the sugar from going straight to the bottom of the bowl. Beat until it is light brown and glossy, maybe 30 seconds. Fold in pecan halves. Using two spoons, drop blobs of the mixture onto either a greased cookie sheet or a cookie sheet with some parchment on it (my preference). Bake for approximately 40 to 50 minutes. My grandma went on the longer end, for really crumbly cookies. I leave them just slightly chewy on the inside - more like 40 to 45 minutes for 2 inch cookies. Let stand for a few minutes before you remove them from the cookie sheet, as they start out a little fragile.

Peach Pie

1 (15 ounce) package pastry for a 9 inch double crust pie
1 egg, beaten
5 cups sliced peeled peaches
2 Tablespoons lemon juice
½ cup all-purpose flour
1 cup white sugar
½ teaspoon ground cinnamon
¼ teaspoon ground nutmeg
¼ teaspoon salt
2 Tablespoons butter

Preheat oven to 450 degrees. Line the bottom and sides of a 9 inch pie plate with one of the pie crusts. Brush with some of the beaten egg to keep the dough from becoming soggy later. Place the sliced peaches in a large bowl, and sprinkle with lemon juice. Mix gently. In a separate bowl, mix together the flour, sugar, cinnamon, nutmeg and salt. Pour over the peaches, and mix gently. Pour into the pie crust, and dot with butter. Cover with the other pie crust, and fold the edges under. Flute the edges to seal or press the edges with the tines of a fork dipped in egg. Brush the remaining egg over the top crust. Cut several slits in the top crust to vent steam. Bake for 10 minutes in the preheated oven, and then reduce the heat to 350 degrees and bake for an additional 30 to 35 minutes, until the crust is brown and the juice begins to bubble through the vents. If the edges brown too fast, cover them with strips of aluminum foil about halfway through baking. Cool before serving. This tastes better warm than hot.

Pear and Brown Sugar Crisp

Topping:
⅔ cup flour
5 Tablespoons butter, softened
¾ cup rolled oats (instant or old-fashioned oatmeal)
½ cup firmly packed dark brown sugar
Pinch salt

Pear Filling:
6 large pears, such as Bosc or Bartlett, cored and cut into 1 inch long by ½ inch thick pieces
1 Tablespoon fresh lemon juice
2 teaspoons vanilla extract
⅓ cup light brown or regular sugar
½ teaspoon ground cinnamon
Pinch ground cloves
4 ½ teaspoons cornstarch

In a food processor, combine the flour, butter, oats, dark brown sugar, and salt. Pulse until the mixture starts to hold together, then set aside. Preheat oven to 350 degrees. In a large bowl, mix pears, lemon juice, vanilla, light brown or regular sugar, cinnamon, cloves, and cornstarch; toss to combine. Pour pear mixture into an 11 by 7 baking dish or 6 individual ramekins. Cover with topping. Turn oven down to 325 degrees and bake the crisp until the top is golden brown and the pears are tender, 70 to 80 minutes. Serve warm or at room temperature.

Kool Aid's Got Thirst on the Run

Summer is here and I am looking forward to hot summer days and planning refreshments for the kids. In my family growing up, pop was a rare treat. Sometimes a trip to Holiday meant we could stock up on their trade mark "Holiday Pop", ten cans for a dollar. These had to be opened with a key can opener and all had names with the word soda in them, like lemon lime soda (I think that would be Sprite today), black cherry soda, root beer soda and cream soda. I swear Gary and I would take ten minutes to pick our favorite flavors only to get them home and argue about who chose what. Friday nights, watching Gilligan's Island, we would sometimes have homemade popcorn and a can of "soda". This was the best night to watch TV because the lineup was great and it ended with "Love American Style". If the neighbors and parents were playing cards they didn't notice if we were up late so it was like we were really getting away with something. I'll bet if I tried I could still sing the theme some from Love American Style or at least hum you a few bars.

Because we were "pop deprived" we moved on to the next best thing. Kool Aid! This sold for ten packs for a dollar but one pack would make a whole 2 quart pitcher. My Grandma Isabelle had these really bright aluminum cups that just made the Kool Aid taste better. (And you could get the Kool Aid really high on your lips and make the best Kool Aid mustaches!) When filled with ice, the cups would sweat and you could write your name in the droplets on the side of the glass. My mom would have us make a pitcher of Kool Aid every night before dinner. In her Tupperware turn a bout canister she kept a one cup measuring scoop. (I swear if you walked in to her house this afternoon you would still see this orange canister set on her counter.) Every time we made Kool Aid she would say "You don't need a whole cup of sugar, only use three fourths of a cup." But we'd keep dumping, stirring and tasting until it was super sweet. Then at dinner she'd make a face and give us "the look". My brother and I liked to re-enact the Kool Aid commercials by yelling "Hey Kool Aid" and taking turns breaking through boxes and stuff. For those of you too young to remember this commercial – check it out on You Tube. (For those of you too old to know about You Tube, never mind, you probably saw the commercials.)

As an adult I still enjoy a glass of Kool Aid on a hot day (Orange is my favorite) but I have found other uses for this beverage drink mix; like fabric dye and play dough. Just for fun you should check out the Kool Aid flavors in the ethnic food isle. Recently I found both mango and pineapple. I didn't try drinking them but they make the best play dough scents and keep the kids guessing. Why the sudden Kool Aid column? Yes there are recipes to follow, but I guarantee the first one is not for the weak at heart. Koolickles! I must be honest and tell you I have not tasted this recipe but I do have a batch brewing in the fridge as I write. If you see me with a red pucker in two weeks you'll know what I've been up to, eating cherry Kool Aid flavored pickles of course! Enjoy summer!

"Love, American Style, Truer than the Red, White and Blue, (ooh ooh), Love, American Style, That's me and you. And on a star spangled night my love, (My love come to me). You can rest your head on my shoulder, Out by the dawn's early light, my love I will defend your right to try. Love, American Style, That's me and you."

Koolickles

Large gallon jar of whole dill pickles
2 cups sugar
Two packets of cherry flavored Kool Aid

Empty pickle juice into large bowl. Remove two cups of juice and discard. Save the rest. Add two cups of sugar and two packets of cherry Kool Aid to pickle juice. Pour "new juice" back over the pickles, cover and refrigerate for two weeks. Enjoy!

Orange Kool Aid Cake

Cake:
1 box white or yellow cake mix
2 teaspoons orange Kool Aid
2 teaspoons vegetable oil

Follow directions on cake box. Plus add Kool Aid and oil. Beat according to directions on box. Bake at 350 degrees.

Frosting:
1 pound powdered sugar
1 teaspoon orange Kool Aid
¼ cup vegetable oil
⅓ cup milk

Beat 2 minutes. Spread on cooled cake.

Kool-Aid Sherbet

1 cup sugar
1 package Kool Aid
3 cups milk

Dissolve sugar and Kool Aid in the milk. Pour into refrigerator freezing tray. Freeze until partially firm. Spoon into cold bowl and beat with an egg beater until smooth but not melted. Return to tray. Freeze until firm, about 2 hours. Makes ¾ quart.

She Served Up More than Fish Sticks

If I asked each and every one of you the following five questions about your childhood, I bet you a dollar you could answer at least four of them right off the top of your head. What was the name of your childhood dog? (Tiny) What street did you live on? (Cramer Road) Who was your very best friend in kindergarten? (Colleen Lamb) What was the color of the carpet in your room? (Green) What was the name of your favorite lunch lady? (Ruby)

I went to grade school at Birch Grove Elementary in Tofte. At that time kids attended classes at Birch Grove kindergarten through the sixth grade. In seventh grade we had to make the long bus ride to Grand Marais where we met kids from all the way up the Gunflint Trail who went to grade school in town and kids from as far as the Canadian border who attended the grade school in Grand Portage. Ruby and Leona, our lunch ladies, served me lunch every school day for seven years. (Except for the ONE DAY I was absent in the third grade, otherwise I had perfect attendance my entire grade school life. Darn ear infection!) Lunches were great. Hot dogs, mashed potatoes and hamburger gravy, we even had pan fried herring from Lake Superior. I really liked the red Jell-O days. Ruby would make it in rimmed baking sheets and then cut it into squares. If it was a special occasion she would dollop each piece with whipping cream. My friend Colleen and I would take a mouthful then tip upside down on the lunch bench and try to swallow "up". Ruby's husband Ray was the janitor and word got out that he was "tipping" another kid a dollar to help him dump and rinse the lunch trays. I stuck around one day to see if I could help out and make a buck but Ray told me to scoot. (I'm pretty sure the money exchanged hands after I was given the boot.)

In Annandale I had the opportunity to work with the lunch ladies of Bendix Elementary for a few weeks. All the women were so nice but I have to tell you one in particular had "rock star" status. Every day the kids "lit up" when she opened the sliding door to serve them. The children loved her and you could tell she really cared about them. She always had a big smile and a laugh that was contagious. They all knew that if it was their birthday they could expect a special treat on their tray. (Some children were too shy to ask for themselves but they all had a "more outgoing" friend who would make sure that word got back to the kitchen.) I was most impressed though; when one of the kids was having a bad day she would stop and take that bit of extra time to see if she could help. (You have to know that means a lot to a kid when you're just trying to get through a tough day at school.) After more than 20 years in the kitchen I'm sure she's heard more than her share of stories, both the good and the bad. It's sad to think about her not being there next year. I know Bendix Elementary will not be the same. I would like to take a moment to toast this special lady and to personally thank her for all the joy she has brought to so many children and adults here in the Annandale Community. Thank you Penny, I wish you all the best!

"To laugh often and much; to win the respect of intelligent people and the affection of children...to leave the world a better place.... to know that even one life has breathed easier because you have lived. This is to have succeeded." ~ Ralph Waldo Emerson

Favorite school lunch recipes.

Toasty Dogs for Two

2 slices bread
Butter
2 slices cheese
2 hot dogs (or veggie dogs)

2 toothpicks

Top each slice of bread with a slice of cheese and a hotdog. Fold over, and secure each with a toothpick. Spread butter on the outside of the bread slices. Toast in toaster oven or regular oven preheated to 350 degrees until golden brown.

Fried Chicken Nuggets

1 pound boneless skinless chicken breast
1 cup flour
¼ teaspoon salt
½ teaspoon paprika
¼ teaspoon pepper
½ teaspoon baking soda

½ cup water
1 Tablespoon vinegar

Fill a pan, electric fry pan, or iron skillet, with oil, leaving about one-inch of pan at the top. Heat the oil to 350 degrees while you prepare the nuggets. Cut up about 1 pound of boneless, skinless, chicken breasts into one-inch pieces. Mix dry ingredients in a small bowl. Add water and vinegar to the dry ingredients. (The vinegar reacts with the baking soda and causes the breading to expand when cooking.) Put a few pieces of chicken into the breading and use tongs to place them in the hot oil. You know the oil is hot when a small piece of bread placed in the oil, rises to the top, sizzles, and starts to brown. After about two minutes turn the nuggets and cook for an additional two minutes on the other side. The nuggets are done when they are golden brown. Serve with ketchup.

Sandy Holthaus

Hot Ham and Cheese Sandwiches

8 to 10 small, crusty rolls
24 to 30 slices Black Forest deli ham
8 to 10 thin slices Swiss cheese
3 Tablespoons Dijon mustard
Aluminum foil

Split rolls in half horizontally. Rolls may be buttered if desired. Place three slices ham and one slice cheese on each roll. Place the roll tops on top of the sandwich and press down lightly. Wrap each sandwich individually in aluminum foil. Stack sandwiches in a crock pot or slow cooker, and turn the heat to low. Cover and cook for about two hours. Serve hot, straight from the slow cooker. Sandwiches can be kept warm on the "low" or "warm" settings for several hours. Makes 8 to 10 sandwiches.

She'll be Coming Around the Mountain When She Comes

This song starts out innocently enough, a visit from a friend, (Yee-ha) but if you know the rest of the song eventually you have to wear scratchy pajamas, sleep with a snoring Grandma and then kill the old red rooster, chop, chop. Welcome to my world.

We have a very mean rooster. In the yard he has attacked the kids on several occasions and one morning he decided he would peck at the back of my legs as I was getting into the van. I swung at him with my purse but if you've ever met a mean rooster you know the minute you turn around they come after you again. Stinker! I hatched the blessed creature from an egg for goodness sake. I turned his egg twice a day for 21 days and greatly anticipated the day he pecked his way from the shell. (I think my time would have been better spent making him into an omelet!)

My boys, Jack and Ben, and my nephew Travis, decided they would save me and "the farm" from future rooster attacks. I was doing the dishes and thinking how peaceful and quiet it was when they came running in the kitchen asking for a BIG knife. Hmmmm....dare I ask? *"What's up boys?"* *"We caught the rooster and now we're going to kill it."* Time to investigate. I headed down to the barn only to see the rooster caught in a fishing net held to the ground with several sticks of fire wood. He DID NOT look happy. *"Well guys what's the plan?"* After much thought they decided they were going to give it a bonk on the head then kill it with the knife. I explained that I personally thought it was wrong to kill an animal unless you planned to eat it and "plucking a chicken" was not on my to-do list that day. *"We'll kill it and bury it in the woods."*(Visions of my mom killing chickens and them running headless around the yard came flooding back to me.) So then I told them that it is a lot harder than you think to kill an animal while looking it in the eye. It's really very sad to take a life. This got them thinking, I could tell, but they weren't backing down. *"We'll just close our eyes while we swing the bat."* This is not what I was getting at guys. (Then I pulled the Karma card.) *"Everything we do in life will eventually come back to us at some point, so if you kill this rooster, someday you might have something sad happen in your life."* Now they looked a little frightened. *"Well boys, I have to do barn chores, you do what you think is best but whatever you decide, do it quick and with as little pain as possible."* When I came out of the barn ten minutes later all three looked sick with guilt; and the rooster, well he looked madder than ever. *"We just couldn't do it Mom".* (Yeah, nothing beats a mother's guilt.)

Now what do I do with a rooster that has just been given a really good reason to attack me? We made a plan to set him free, just not in the yard where he can get come after us. Together we decided the best way is to gently and peacefully "move him off the farm" with a little drive down the road and into the woods. He might have been hatched in an incubator but now he's "born free" (or as my husband calls him "Fox food".) Ah the circle of life.

> *"I would never disrespect any man, woman, "rooster" or child out there. We're all the same. What goes around comes around, and karma kicks us all in the butt in the end of the day." - Angie Stone*

If you do decide to "kill the old red rooster" here are some ideas on how to cook him up.

Reddened Rooster

3 to 4 pound rooster cut in pieces
1 cup olive oil

2 teaspoons of salt
½ teaspoon pepper
½ cup red wine
½ cup chopped tomatoes
½ Tablespoon tomato paste
5 to 6 cloves garlic, minced
2 medium onions, minced
10 to 12 pearl onions, whole
2 pounds potatoes, peeled, cut in large chunks
2 to 3 whole cloves
1 bay leaf
1 small stick cinnamon
8 to 10 cups water

In a skillet, heat the oil over high heat and brown the meat quickly. Transfer the meat to a stew pot, and in the remaining oil, sauté the pearl onions until slightly soft. Set the pearl onions aside, and in the same oil, sauté the minced garlic and onions. When the onions soften, add chopped tomatoes. Dissolve the tomato paste in the wine and add to the pan. Stir well to blend and cook at boiling for 5 to 7 minutes. Add the sauce to the stew pot on top of the meat, and turn heat to high. Stir in salt, pepper, bay leaf, and cinnamon stick. Add 1 cup of the water and bring to a boil. Stir in remaining water slowly. When full boil resumes, cover, reduce heat to medium, and cook for 30 minutes. Add pearl onions, and cook for 30 minutes more. Add potatoes and cook for the final 30 minutes. Test meat for doneness.

Corfu Rooster

1 rooster, cut into pieces
7 garlic cloves, smashed
1 teaspoon cinnamon
1 teaspoon salt
½ teaspoon black pepper

3 Tablespoon olive oil
1 Tablespoon tomato paste
2 Tablespoons red wine vinegar (or cider vinegar)
2 medium onions, halved and thinly sliced
3 ½ cups water
½ cup dry white wine
1 teaspoon sugar

Pat chicken dry. Stir together cinnamon, salt, pepper and sprinkle over the chicken. Heat oil in a skillet and brown chicken in two batches on all sides, transfer to a plate meanwhile, stir tomato paste and vinegar. Add more oil to skillet if necessary and sauté onions till golden; about 6 minutes. Stir in tomato mixture and simmer 1 minute. Stir in water, wine sugar and simmer uncovered, 5 minutes. Add chicken to pot and simmer, covered, until tender (1 to 3 hours, depending on how tough your rooster is). Transfer cooked chicken to a platter and boil sauce, uncovered, till reduced to about 2 ½ cups (about 10 minutes). Season with salt!

Red Roosters in a glass (My personal favorite)

1 ½ quart cranberry juice cocktail
1 (6 ounce) can frozen orange juice concentrate, defrosted
2 cups vodka
Hold the rooster.

Combine all of the ingredients in a large plastic container. Freeze for several hours. It will not freeze solid, but rather achieve the consistency of a slushy. Scoop into punch cups or wine glasses and serve.

Can a Ham Sandwich
lead you to Heaven??

I was raised by parents who, by example, are really good neighbors. At the drop of a hat I remember them helping out friends and strangers alike. Whether it be a burning house, (and there were several of these as most people heated with wood stoves), or someone sick, my mom and dad offered to help out in any way they could. Back in the days of CB radios my mom stayed up all night once helping travelers find their way around a flooded Highway 61 using back roads so they could get home. Her handle was the "Lazy Lady". My dad would bring home stranded travelers to spend the night until they could get their cars fixed. More than once I remember stepping over sleeping strangers on our living room floor and sharing my breakfast with people I'd never met. They are just the kind of people who like to help out. Of course this goes both ways, they have great neighbors who are there when my parents need a hand too.

I thought of this the other day when I was discussing religion with a friend. (I know taboo, sort of like politics, but I like to ride the edge.) I said I loved God, but not religion. I developed this theory at an early age. As a child of about ten I attended church with a friend for fun one weekend. At this particular church the pastor said attendance to Sunday service was a must. If you didn't go to church you would go to hell, it was as simple as that. I found this to be a very scary thought as it is well known to this day my dad limits his church attendance to baptisms, wedding and funerals. This bothered me for weeks until I talked it over with my Grandma Barb, another neighbor whom I love and respect. She said that was the silliest thing she ever heard.

She told me "Good people go to heaven because they are good people not because they check in every Sunday like roll call." This one statement changed my view in religion forever.

My husband and I want to be good neighbors like my parents but so far no homes have burned in our area (thank goodness) and CB radios are now antiques, so we jumped at the chance when we got a call from our neighbor who needed help with her vacuum. "Jersey Girl" is an east coast transplant and let's just say "Little House on the Prairie" was not her favorite show. All these Minnesota wild animals, with the exception of bunnies, give her the shivers. It seemed she had accidently sucked up a mouse with her Dyson vacuum cleaner and now the little dead creature was making a terrible stink. She couldn't watch as we carefully unscrewed the bottom of the vacuum cleaner. I was a little squeamish myself but Mike took the lead and started taking the vacuum apart. There it was, not a mouse but a much mangled Ham Sandwich! I have to admit the smell was something awful. We brought it in the house to show her "the kill". She will never live this down. City girl sucks up a ham sandwich! But hey we were there for her, being good neighbors and all.

> *If a man wrote a better book, a preach a better sermon, or*
> *if he'd make a better mouse-trap than his neighbor, though*
> *he builds his house in the woods, the world will make a*
> *beaten path to his door." ~ Ralph Waldo Emerson*

Good ideas for ham other than making sandwhiches…...

Crock Pot Black Eyed Peas and Ham

1 pound frozen black eyed peas
1 cup chicken broth
2 ribs celery, thinly sliced
4 cloves garlic, minced
1 bunch (6 to 8) green onions, thinly sliced

6 ounces diced ham
½ teaspoon coarsely ground black pepper
½ teaspoon Creole seasoning

Combine all ingredients in slow cooker. Cover and cook on LOW for 6 to 8 hours.

Ham and Pickle Roll Ups

3 packages cream cheese, softened
1 pound ham, thinly sliced
1 quart whole dill pickles, drained, patted dry.

Place pickles on a paper towel to dry off some of the juice. Carefully spread the cream cheese on a 2 slices of ham. Roll a pickle up in the ham slice and roll again with the other ham slice. Slice into one-inch pieces. Repeat as necessary. Refrigerate at least 2 hours before serving.

Deep Dish Ham Pie

¼ cup butter
¼ cup all-purpose flour
½ teaspoon salt
¼ teaspoon ground mustard
⅛ teaspoon pepper
1 cup milk
1 teaspoon dried minced onion
2 ½ cups fully cooked ham, cubed
1 cup frozen peas, thawed
2 hardboiled eggs, chopped
Pastry for single crust pie, 8 inch

Melt butter in saucepan; stir in flour, salt mustard and pepper until smooth. Gradually add milk and onion; bring to a boil, stirring constantly. Continue cooking and stirring for about 2 minutes longer, until thickened. Stir in ham, peas and hardboiled eggs. Pour mixture into an eight-inch square or round baking dish. On a floured surface, roll pastry to fit top of dish; place over filling. Seal and crimp edges; cut slits in the top. Bake at 425 degrees for 25 minutes or until crust is golden brown and filling is bubbly.

Long Live the Queen!

You can dress her up but she's still a zucchini!

I love attending farmers markets this time of year. There is such a variety of booths I often don't know where to start, and this year we have two great markets in our area, the Kimball Farmers Market on Fridays and the Annandale Farmers Market on Saturday. One Friday night I bought these wonderful frozen apple torts. I baked them at home and served with fresh made whipped cream! (Really good!) Then I made some meatballs and used with homemade BBQ sauce I also purchased at the market. They make it with a touch of honey from their own bee hives; this BBQ sauce is so good you can eat it right out of the jar. We also bought fresh granola and corn on the cob. There was not a zucchini in site, I was so impressed. (I happen to know that zucchinis are out there lurking though....I tripped over a box my BFF left in the church doorway a couple of weeks ago.) (I'd take them for compost but the darn things would probably try to multiply while rotting so I don't even risk it.)

Early Saturday morning I headed out. I bought fresh tomatoes from Abe's booth and a deep purple eggplant from Amy. I planned to make grilled eggplant served with basmati rice. Fresh raspberries and a dozen of Papa Tom's cookies rounded out the shopping bag. I even spoiled myself with some scented goats milk soaps. I truly was in heavenly bliss. Could life get any better??? Yes my friend it could... with a loaf fresh bread! I went home and quickly toasted the bread and made a BLT sandwich. As I sat down at the kitchen table I suddenly had the feeling of being watched.....I thought I was home alone....I looked out the patio window and screamed...what in the world was that??? When I realized it was a giant zucchini I screamed again! I knew the day would come when the queen of the most despised vegetable would finally hunt me down. What could she possible want?? It turns out she wanted to give me a note (or more Queenly, a scroll)

It read: Queen Z so declares: "Don't be a Weenie and malign the glorious zucchini...fatted, fried or baked, we're wonderful in cake! Put us in a salad for a complexion rosy, not pallid. Because we're quite prolific share us with all neighbors. You needn't be specific. If you do this all then you'll agree, Zucchini is Terrific!" Love, Queen Z

Clearly this is one deranged produce! If I were to cook her up and feed her to the neighbors, the Queen would be sentencing her own execution! Oh well, who am I to disobey a Queen? – OFF WITH HER HEAD! (I promise to treat her royally with these delicious recipes!) PS. Only my sweet neighbor would even *think* to give a zucchini a crown and a belly button for goodness sake. She is soooo busted!

Favorite Queen Quote:
"Fool! Don't you see now that I could have poisoned you a hundred times had I been able to live without you." ~ Cleopatra

Zucchini Tini

1 Tablespoon zucchini water

Note: To make zucchini water, grate a large zucchini into a fine mesh strainer set over a bowl. Then toss the grated zucchini with a pinch of coarse salt and allow it to sit for 15 minutes. The grated zucchini then can be pressed (using hands or the back of a sturdy wooden spoon) to extract the water.

$\frac{1}{4}$ cup unfiltered cold sake or vodka
$\frac{1}{8}$ cup gin
1 thin slice of zucchini, for garnish

In a cocktail shaker, combine the zucchini water, sake or vodka and gin. Fill the shaker with ice, then shake well and strain into a chilled cocktail glass. Garnish with the zucchini slice.

Zucchini "Crab" Cakes

2 $\frac{1}{2}$ cups zucchini, grated
1 cup bread crumbs, fine
1 egg, beaten
2 Tablespoons butter, melted
1 Tablespoon Old Bay seasoning
4 Tablespoons flour
1 small onion, chopped fine
Oil and margarine or butter for frying

This recipe is only good when the squash are fresh...frozen squash doesn't work. Mix all ingredients together until well blended.

Shape into patties. Fry in a mixture of half oil/half margarine until golden on each side. Turn only once. Drain on paper towels. Serve hot, with cocktail sauce on the side.

Orange Zucchini Cake

1 cup flour
1 teaspoon baking powder
½ teaspoon baking soda
¼ teaspoon salt
1 teaspoon ground cinnamon
½ teaspoon ground nutmeg
¾ cup sugar
½ cup vegetable oil
2 eggs
½ cup All Bran cereal
1 ½ teaspoon of grated orange peel
1 teaspoon of vanilla
1 cup of grated zucchini
½ cup chopped nuts
½ cup raisins

Combine flour, baking powder, soda, salt, cinnamon and nutmeg. Set aside. In a large bowl, beat sugar, oil and eggs until combined. Stir in cereal, orange peel and vanilla. Add flour mixture, zucchini, nuts and raisins. Spread evenly in greased 10 by 6 glass pan. Bake at 325 degrees for 35 minutes or until toothpick comes out clean. Cool completely and spread with cream cheese frosting.

Do you see what I see?

Zoë took this picture of a "loon cloud" over
Lake John, Annandale, MN

The last days of summer, just before school starts, I remember as being lonely times for me growing up. I would miss my "town" friends, because I lived 36 miles away on the West End. I was bored, bored, bored but dared not say so or mom would find chores to keep me occupied. Sometimes I had to be creative to find something to do. I had a best friend, Colleen Lamb, who lived only a mile away, and we would play this game of looking up at the clouds and try to see the same cloud, she at her house by Lake Superior and me one mile inland. Believe it or not sometimes it worked. I distinctly remember a cloud that looked like Richard

Nixon, the early years. Hey, Colleen saw it too. I thought of this when my daughter Zoë showed me a picture of a perfect "loon cloud" she had taken over Lake John near Annandale. I had to share it with you. Is there a chance someone else saw this cloud??? That would be really special.

My daughter Zoë is not only a talented photographer she is now a world traveler. In 2010 she left to spend the next three weeks in Australia. While driving to the airport it occurred to me that it was 16 years ago to the day that I was bringing her home from the hospital as a newborn baby. Now she was flying half way around the world? What was I doing? My friends, it's called a huge "leap of faith". I started to get teary eyed at the thought but then my two boys made me promise not to embarrass them by crying at the check in gate. I wondered what she would see in the Australian sky. The same sun and moon, only 15 hours before we do, but what about the sky, what about the clouds? An Aussie might see this bird shaped cloud but they probably wouldn't call it a "Loon Cloud", which it quite obviously is; I bet they might call it "Kookaburra Cloud". (Hey don't laugh; we named ours "Loon" for goodness sake.)

Daughter Zoë, her friend Chloe and a Kuala in Sydney, Australia

Like our children, the sky is an amazing gift we receive each and every day. And like our children it is constantly moving and changing forms. One day a baby in my arms with a head full of beautiful hair and the next day waving goodbye at the gate on her way around the world. She may grow up and "fly" away but her smile is the same. Always beautiful, trusting, full of hope and wonderful to look at, just like the sky. Ok now I'm crying all over again. (I'll try not to embarrass you.) Let's celebrate Zoë's travels with some Australian Cuisine.

"The sky is the daily bread of the eyes". Ralph Waldo Emerson

Damper

Damper is the bush-bread of Australia. Drovers baked Damper in camp ovens buried in the hot ashes of their camp fires in the Outback, but if you don't want to build a camp fire in your backyard, damper can also be baked in a normal kitchen oven.

4 cups self-rising flour
½ teaspoon salt
1 ½ cups milk
Butter
Extra flour

Sift the flour and salt into a bowl and make a well in the middle. Pour in the milk and mix. Grease the camp oven or round baking pan and dust with flour. Place dough in the camp oven or pan. Cut a cross in the top surface of dough. Close lid of camp oven and bake in the hot ashes of your camp fire for about 30 minutes, or bake in preheated normal kitchen oven for thirty minutes at 425 degrees. Eat with a cup of tea, boiled in a billy. (Don't ask me what a billy might be, I don't know.)

Pikelets

Pikelets are little scone like treats usually served with coffee or tea.

1 cup flour
1 teaspoon cream of tartar
½ teaspoon soda
1 egg
Few drops lemon flavoring
2 Tablespoons sugar
Milk as needed

Sift the first 3 ingredients together in a bowl, and then add sugar. Make a well in the center of the mixture and drop in egg and some milk. Mix from center, gathering flour from the sides of the well. Add milk as needed to make a thick batter. Add a few drops of lemon essence to taste. Drop batter into hot frying pan to make 3" circles. Top with butter or jam.

Dinkum Chili (Beef)

½ pound bacon
2 Tablespoons oil
2 onions, medium, coarsely chopped
1 celery stalk, coarsely chopped
1 bell pepper, seeded and chopped
2 pounds top beef sirloin, cut into 1" cubes
1 pound hamburger
1 pound ground pork
3 Tablespoons ground red Chile
2 garlic cloves, medium, fine chopped
1 Tablespoon dried oregano
1 Tablespoon cumin, ground
2 (12 ounce) cans beer, (preferably Australian)
1 (15 ounce) can whole tomatoes
3 Tablespoons brown sugar
1 Boomerang

Fry the bacon in a skillet over medium heat. Drain the strips on paper towels, dice and reserve. Heat the oil in a large heavy pot over medium heat. Add the onions, celery, and green pepper and cook until the onions are translucent. Combine all the beef and pork with the ground Chile, garlic, oregano, and cumin. Add this meat and spice mixture to the pot. Break up any lumps with a fork and cook, stirring occasionally, until the meat is evenly browned. Add the beer, tomatoes, and reserved bacon to the pot. Bring to a boil, and then lower the heat and simmer, uncovered, for 1 ½ hours. Wave a boomerang over the pot 14 times each hour from this point on. (This is definitely optional adding no noticeable flavor, just a touch of authenticity and fun.) Stir for 3 minutes. Taste, adjust seasonings, and add more beer if desired. Simmer for 2 ½ hours longer. Add the brown sugar and simmer for 15 minutes longer, vigorously waving the boomerang over the pot. Makes 8 servings.

I Am Soup

As I celebrated my birthday last October, I started to feel a little old. Not just older but old. Because, unless I plan to live beyond the age of 92, I am now on the "downhill slide." My friends, I have now lived at least 50% of my life. This is a concept that I found hard to get my head around. I began to feel I'm spread a little too thin, watered down and maybe, just maybe, somewhat drab. Kind of like leftovers in the fridge, not yet spoiled but maybe not the most appetizing either. Hmmmmm....I know what you're thinking. Buck up kiddo! You are way too young to feel this way. I know you're right; I needed a Woman Wellness Weekend. It came just in time. Besides you and I both know the best thing to do with old leftovers is to make soup.

That Friday night I headed up to the Audubon Center in Sandstone to meet my sister-cousin, my auntie from Vegas and my mom for a three day of "Pull me out of my day old funk" weekend. It started with a good healthy dinner followed by a speaker who led us through "Love the Skin you're in." It was all about finding the best in ourselves. (That added a little meat to the broth.) The next day in "Guided Imagery through Music" I drew a beautiful mandalas of birds and a flower. A mandalas is a circular drawing that is very meditative. (This really added some soothing spices to my soup.) Then I made a nature scrapbook out of recycled paper bags. Talk about fun. My aunt kept thinking she lacked creativity so she would try to get me to decorate her pages for her but then she would tell me her ideas were better than mine. She actually has a good eye but she lacks glue stick abilities. Then we made facials with chocolate, coffee grounds and real cream. Ok I know it sounds gross, and I have the pictures to prove it, but my skin has never been so smooth. (These classes represent the freshest veggies available to add flavor to my soup.)

By Saturday night I was really starting to feel like a new person. After a presentation on Acupuncture we gathered for singing around the fireplace. I know you're expecting old campfire songs like Kumbaya but we sang songs of joy and empowerment. For example "I Will Survive" and "Proud Mary". One woman, who shared her age as 71, was up and dancing around like Tina Turner. It was lots of smiles and fun. We ate S'mores and drank red wine. I highly recommend this combination. The weekend ended with a hot stone massage, a birthday gift from my sweet mother. (This had to be the dumplings and carrots of the soup, my favorite ingredients by the way.) I was fully recovered, as soup. It's a good feeling. I now like to think of myself as a warm, nurturing bowl of soup ready to feed my family and friends. Most of all I learned that I have to remember to feed myself so I can feed others.

PS. Of course there is always a secret ingredient to any good homemade soup, in my case it is hard belly laughter. I found this special ingredient the Fred Eaglesmith concert in South Haven. His music, stories and jokes were just what the doctor ordered. I wiped the tears of laughter from my eyes several times.

> *"Good soup is one of the prime ingredients of good living.*
> *For soup can do more to lift the spirits and stimulate the*
> *appetite than any other one dish." ~ Louis P. De Gouy*

Chocolate Chili

1 pound ground beef (or a veggie alternative)
1 cup chopped onion
1 cup hot water
2 (14.5 ounce) cans diced tomatoes with garlic, undrained
1 (15 ounce) can kidney beans, rinsed and drained
1 (15 ounce) can black beans, rinsed and drained

1 (14.5 ounce) can whole kernel corn, drained
⅓ cup semisweet chocolate chips
2 teaspoons chili powder
1 Tablespoon ground cumin
½ teaspoon dried oregano
1 teaspoon salt

Combine ground beef and onion in a large saucepan over medium-high heat. Cook, stirring, until beef is browned, about 5 minutes. Transfer cooked beef and onions to slow cooker. Stir in water, tomatoes, kidney beans, black beans, corn, chocolate chips, chili powder, cumin, oregano, and salt. Cook on High until chili begins to bubble, about 20 minutes. Reduce heat to low, and cook until thick, about 2 hours.

Red-Pepper Soup with Basil Cream

3 cloves garlic, chopped
1 small onion, chopped
2 Tablespoons olive oil
1 can (15 ounce) crushed tomatoes
1 jar (12 ounce) marinated roasted red peppers, drained and chopped
2 cups chicken broth
½ cup packed fresh basil
1 Tablespoon balsamic vinegar
2 teaspoons sugar
¼ cup sour cream
¼ cup heavy cream
¼ cup chopped fresh basil, for basil cream
½ teaspoon salt
½ teaspoon freshly ground pepper

Sauté garlic and onion with olive oil in large pot over medium heat for 6 minutes. Add tomatoes, red peppers, and chicken broth.

Cook for 15 minutes. Add fresh basil, balsamic vinegar, and sugar and puree in a blender or food processor. For basil cream, stir sour cream and heavy cream together with chopped basil and salt and freshly ground pepper. Serve soup with dollop of basil cream and a garnish of chopped basil.

Roasted Garlic Soup

4 bulbs garlic, whole
¼ cup olive oil
6 Tablespoons butter
4 leeks, chopped
1 onion, chopped
6 Tablespoons flour
4 cups chicken broth
⅓ cup dry sherry
1 cup heavy whipping cream
1 Tablespoon lemon juice, or to taste
Salt to taste
¼ teaspoon freshly ground white pepper
2 Tablespoons chopped fresh chives

Cut off top ¼ inch of each garlic head. Place in a small, shallow baking dish. Drizzle olive oil over cloves. Bake at 350 degrees until golden, about 1 hour. Cool slightly. Press individual garlic cloves between thumb and finger to release. Chop garlic. Melt butter or margarine in heavy large saucepan over medium heat. Add garlic, leeks, and onion; sauté until onion is translucent, about 8 minutes. Add flour and cook 10 minutes, stirring occasionally. Stir in hot broth and sherry. Simmer 20 minutes, stirring occasionally. Cool slightly. Puree soup in batches in a blender or food processor. Return soup to saucepan, and add cream. Simmer until thickened, about 10 minutes. Add lemon juice to taste. Season with salt and white pepper. Laddle into bowls. Garnish with chives.

Pancakes Anyone?

When I visit the post office to mail packages I struggle against looking guilty when they ask "Does your package contain anything fragile, liquid, perishable, or hazardous?" I personally have not mailed any such items but I must admit I did receive them, twice, from my mother, prior to the 9/11 rule being imposed of course. Don't get me wrong my mother didn't intentionally send me something that would blow up in my Coon Rapids mailbox on that hot summer day. It just kinda happened. Her heart was in the right place and I did call her and ask her for the item, I just never dreamed she would MAIL IT. What in the world? You might ask. Yes, my friend, she *mailed* me sour dough starter!

Just for a moment, let's go back. My mother has had sour dough starter in her refrigerator since 1971. If you were to visit my mom this weekend I can almost guarantee you would be treated to her famous sourdough pancakes for breakfast. They are thin and delicious. (Even better with Grandma Barb's homemade maple syrup.) She mixes up the batter the night before and our mouths start to water because we know we will wake up to the smell of frying pancakes. My sons are now at the age where they brag on how many pancakes they can eat in one sitting. Both are usually well on their way past eight pancakes before they groan and push back from the table. My husband is no better. He will sit and wait for plate after plate of fresh pancakes to pass under his nose. You won't believe this but I have never once sat down to pancakes with my mom in my entire life. She doesn't have time to eat! She has to stand and fry them two at a time at her gas stove. (She wouldn't have an *electric* stove if you threw it at her. "Can't regulate the heat" she says. And don't you dare mention an electric griddle; you won't hear the end of it.)

If you don't have sour dough starter in your fridge or don't know about sour dough, here's the secret: to keep the starter going you have to <u>use it</u>. (Kind of like exercise, use it or lose it.) Well, I have lost it, more than once. In mom's words "You killed the starter again." She makes it sound like a homicide. It's my fault; she has warned me again and again. "Sandy, you have to mix it up at least once a month to keep it going." Well just days after I told her I killed my starter, I went to the mailbox to collect my mail when I noticed an odd smell coming from the metal box, as I pried open the door I was shocked to find the entire inside of my mailbox covered in white, doughy goo. At first I thought it was a prank. Then I found the ruptured package and a sweet note from my mom, "Dear Sandy, I have kept starter going for more than 30 years, do you think you could try to keep it alive for an easy year or two? Love, Mom." It was like a shot across the bow. A warning....kill it again and next time it won't be sour dough in the mail box, it will be boiled Easter eggs mailed to your office. (But that, my friend, is another story...I did say she mailed explosives twice didn't I?)

> *"In a big family the first child is kind of like the first pancake. If it's not perfect, that's okay, there are a lot more coming along."*~ Antonin Scalia

Homemade Sour Dough Starter

2 cups whole milk
2 cups flour

Let the milk set in a warm place such as sunny window uncovered to sour. Add the sour milk to the flour preferably in a crock or clay bowl. It is OK to mix the fresh milk and flour but it might take a day or so longer to get a good starter. Cover with cheesecloth and let stand in a warm place (70 to 80 degrees) stirring occasionally. When ready the starter should have a sour smell with small bubbles gently rising to the surface. The whole process will take from 5 to 10 days depending the time of year. Place in a jar and refrigerate.

Sour Dough for Recipes

Place your starter in a glass bowl and add one cup milk and one cup of all purpose flour. Loosely cover with a towel and let set on the counter overnight or at least eight hours. If you have company or your recipe calls for more than two cups of starter, double the amount of milk and the amount of flour added to the starter. When mixing up for pancakes in the morning remember to also double the other ingredients.

First thing in the morning or after batter sits for eight hours, stir batter and put one about one cup of starter back in your starter jar. If you skip this step your starter is gone!

Sour Dough Pancakes

Once you have removed one cup of starter, add to the remainder, one egg, one Tablespoon oil, one Tablespoon sugar, one teaspoon baking soda and once teaspoon salt. Fry as pancakes or cook in a waffle iron. Delicious with fresh picked wild blueberries and maple syrup.

Melt in your mouth Sour Dough Biscuits

The sourdough starter adds a tang and some leavening to these homey biscuits.

1 cup Sourdough Starter
¼ cup cooking oil
1½ cups flour
¼ teaspoon baking soda

Sandy Holthaus

¼ teaspoon salt
Melted butter (optional)
Dillseed OR dried herb (optional)

In a mixing bowl, combine the Sourdough Starter and cooking oil. Add the all-purpose flour, baking soda, and salt. On a lightly floured surface, knead dough gently for 10 to 12 strokes. Roll or pat dough to half-inch thickness. Cut with a two and a half inch biscuit cutter, flouring the cutter after each biscuit. Transfer biscuits to a baking sheet. Bake in a 425 degree oven for 8 to 10 minutes OR until golden brown. If you like, brush with melted butter and sprinkle lightly with dill seed OR dried herb. Serve warm. Makes 12 biscuits.

A Cup Full of Love

As Valentine's Day grows near, one starts to think of Love. In my case I decorate our house for the season with heart shaped soaps in the bathroom and homemade heart art projects placed around the rest of the house. I even get out the old Underwood typewriter with stationary in case anyone would like to type a little love note the old fashioned way. Without spell-check and a printer. You even have to use the backspace to make an exclamation point so you know they really mean it if you get a letter with lots of !!!!!'s. But just where is the best place to look for love? My "Jersey-Girl" friend found love in a low fat Soy Latte at the In Hot Water coffee house a couple of weeks ago. When the cup came to her, there it was, a perfect heart floating in the froth. Then it stayed! You could still see the heart at the bottom of the cup just waiting to put a smile on her face. It was "A Hug in a Mug". I thought it was magic.

In grade school you found love in the boy on the playground who was most likely to hit you, because everyone knows that is how young boys show their affection. A gentle shove would not do it because that might just be a sign of irritation. (I was poked in the eye on the jungle gym once, but my head might have just gotten in the way; he was really aiming for the girl next to me.) By high school you knew it was love if a boy took the time to dial all seven of the numbers on the phone and call you. He might not say too much…lots of silent mind reading and small talk…but in your heart you knew it was love simply because he called. Some of my best memories are of talking (or not talking) on the phone for hours on end with that special someone. Just knowing we were connected across the miles by a phone line….ear to ear….it just doesn't get much better than that. A good Love Note could make or break the deal as well. Here's an old favorite..."Dear Sandy I really, really, really like you. (Yeah!) P.S. I am sorry I kissed your best friend this summer." (What the...?)"

I now look for love in heart shaped rocks. I find them along the shoreline or the driveway. I also like rocks with a heart shape drawn through the veins. Last March I found the perfect rock to give my husband for our anniversary along the shore of Lake Superior east of town by Croftville. Yes I was the crazed woman wading ankle deep in freezing waters just to find the one I wanted. (It took two Bloody Marys and a Lightning Lemonade at the old bank building to get the feeling back in my toes but it was worth it.) I am sure that every time he sees that rock sitting in front of the fireplace he thinks WOW, she's crazy but she really loves me.

Let us all agree to show our love for that someone special this year, be it in a cup of Soy Latte, a phone call, a rock, or a special love note (minus the confession of indiscretion!). With my heart, I wish you all the best!

"God gave us: Two hands to hold. Two legs to walk. Two eyes to see. Two ears to listen. But why give us only one heart? Because he gave the other to someone else, for us to find." ~ Unknown

Sweet Dreams Soup

1 small potato, peeled and chopped
2 Tablespoons butter
1 cup leeks, chopped
2 large carrots, finely chopped
⅛ teaspoon powdered ginger
¼ teaspoon thyme
⅛ teaspoon nutmeg
¼ teaspoon salt
½ teaspoon pepper
One stalk celery, chopped

2 ½ cups milk
Croutons for garnish

Boil the potato in 2 cups of water until tender, about 15 minutes. Drain, save the broth, and set the potato aside. Melt the butter in a soup pot on medium heat. Add the leek, half of the carrots, ginger, thyme, nutmeg, salt, and pepper. Sauté for 5 minutes, stirring with a wooden spoon. Add the celery, the remaining carrots, the cooked potato, and the potato broth. Add 1 cup water, and stir. Bring to a boil, and then reduce heat and simmer, covered, until the carrots are tender, about 20 minutes. In a blender or a bowl, blend or mash 2 cups of the soup with the milk until thick and silky smooth. Return the blended soup to the soup pot, and stir. Ladle into bowls and garnish.

Brownie Kisses

1 package (1 pound 3.8 ounces) fudge brownie mix
¼ cup water
½ cup vegetable oil
2 eggs
1 ¼ cups vanilla milk chips
About 25 milk chocolate kisses with white chocolate stripes, unwrapped
1 ½ teaspoons shortening

Heat oven to 350 degrees. Grease bottom only of spring form pan, 9 by 3 inches deep. Stir brownie mix, water, oil, eggs and 1 cup of the vanilla milk chips in medium bowl about 50 strokes with spoon or until well blended. Spread in pan. Bake 35 to 40 minutes or until toothpick inserted 2 inches from side of pan comes out clean or almost clean. Immediately place chocolate kisses around outside edge of brownie. Cool completely. Remove side of pan.

Place remaining one fourth cup vanilla milk chips and the

shortening in resealable plastic sandwich bag; seal. Microwave on High about 30 seconds or until chips are melted. Knead chips until smooth. Cut small corner from bag. Drizzle melted chips over top of brownie. Cut into wedges.

Exotic Love Tea

1 cup water
¼ cup honey
1 cup apple juice
¼ teaspoon cinnamon
6 Celestial Seasonings Cranberry Cove Tea Bags

Bring water and juice to a boil. Stir in honey and cinnamon. Add the tea bags. Remove from heat. Let stand for one hour. Add 6 cups cold water. Pour into glasses with ice. Sit back, sip and fall in love. Can be stored in the refrigerator for three days.

Baby, You're A Character!

The love of reading started for me really early, probably by the second grade. Until now I hadn't realized the effect all this reading had on my life even, if possibly, some of it was subliminal. After close evaluation, it would appear that all of my children have names from characters in some of my favorite books. This realization came to me with the recent death of J.D. Salinger. I knew from the beginning that my daughter, Zoë was named from his book Franny and Zooey. Although not my favorite Salinger book, I liked the name Zooey from the first time I read the title. I preferred the spelling Zoë though as I thought Zooey would be accidently pronounce Zoo-ie (Like a zoo.) and I thought the simpler spelling with oomlouts (two dots over the "e") looked nicer. My favorite Salinger book is his most famous: "The Catcher in the Rye." (Zoë was very close to being named Phoebe until my mother objected.) The first time I discovered this book I was about 13, visiting my grandparents in Washington State. While riding across the Puget Sound on a ferry boat a young girl was laying on the deck laughing hysterically at the book she was reading. I thought…I have got to read that book so I took a peek at the title, The Catcher in the Rye. I too laughed out loud when I read the story. It's a good book to re-read every few years because I think the story changes with your age and your point of view.

My very favorite books at Birch Grove Elementary School were The Boxcar Children written by Gertrude Chandler Warner. I wanted to BE a boxcar child. I wanted to live in the woods and make scrambled eggs over an open fire and solve mysteries with my clever mind. These books are the best and not until a few days ago did I remember that the youngest boy was named "Benny". Could this have led to the naming of my son Ben??? It's certainly possible. The adventures of Henry, Jessie, Violet and Benny gave me hours and hours of entertainment as a child. I now own the actual books from the elementary library. Some of the books still have the original library cards in them. My name, Sandy Anderson, is scrawled on the checked out by line dated 1973.

By now I bet you're wondering which book inspired the name of my fun loving son, named Jack??? For this I really had to think....I knew there was a character named Jack somewhere, somehow in all of the hundreds of books I read as a child. Then it came to me...Laura Ingalls Wilder! The Little House Books! These were really fun to read. I especially liked "Little House in the Big Woods" because they made maple syrup just like we did when I was young, cooking the sap over an open wood fire outside in the yard. Trust me there is nothing better than homemade maple syrup. Did you know it takes over 40 gallons of maple tree sap to make ONE gallon of syrup??? That's a whole lot of sap. Anyway, can you place the character Jack in the Little House books? He was their beloved dog! Great names have to come from somewhere and I do love dogs as we now have five. Peace, a good book, and delicious cooking to you!

"Show me the books he loves and I shall know the man far better than through mortal friends" ~ *Dawn Adams*

Swedish "Catcher In The Rye" Cookies

1 cup rye flour
1 cup all purpose flour
½ teaspoon salt
½ cup cream cheese, room temperature
½ cup butter, room temperature
½ cup sugar
Large grain sugar (for sprinkling)
Powdered sugar (for snow)

Line two baking sheets with parchment paper. In a medium-sized bowl combine the flours and salt. Set aside. With an electric mixer (or by hand) beat the cream cheese until light and fluffy, add the butter and do the same, mixing until the two are well combined. Beat in the sugar and mix until well incorporated. Add the flour mixture to the butter mixture and stir only long enough to combine the two. The dough should no longer be dusty looking. Turn the dough out onto the counter, knead once or twice to bring it together, shape into a ball, flatten, wrap in plastic and chill it in a refrigerator for two hours. Heat oven to 350 degrees, and arrange the racks in the top and bottom thirds. When you are ready to roll out your cookies do so on a lightly floured work surface. Roll the dough out to quarter-inch thickness, and cut into shapes with the cookie cutter of your choice. Place on the prepared baking sheets an inch apart, and sprinkle each cookie with a bit of large grain sugar. Bake for six or seven minutes, just until cookies are fragrant, and getting a bit golden at the edges. Avoid over baking or they will come out on the dry side. Allow to cool, and dust cookies with a bit of powdered sugar.

Perfect "Boxcar" Scrambled Eggs

Making the perfect scrambled eggs isn't difficult. The key is whisking the eggs thoroughly and vigorously before cooking them. And fluffier is better! Overcooking is a common problem with scrambled eggs. The perfect scrambled eggs should be soft and just a little bit moist. Eggs should be cooked in a nonstick sauté pan. Use a heat resistant rubber spatula.

8 eggs
½ cup whole milk
2 Tablespoons butter
Salt and pepper, to taste

Crack the eggs into a glass mixing bowl and beat them until they turn a pale yellow color. Heat a heavy nonstick sauté pan over medium-low heat. Add the butter and let it melt. Add the milk to the eggs and season to taste with salt and pepper. Then, grab your whisk and whisk like crazy. You're going to want to work up a sweat here. If you're not up for that, you can use an electric beater or stand mixer with the whisk attachment. Whatever device you use, you're trying to beat as much air as possible into the eggs. When the butter in the pan is hot enough to make a drop of water hiss, pour in the eggs. Don't stir! Let the eggs cook for up to a minute or until the bottom starts to set. With a heat resistant rubber spatula, gently push one edge of the egg into the center of the pan, while tilting the pan to allow the still liquid egg to flow in underneath. Repeat with the other edges, until there's no liquid left. Turn off the heat and continue gently stirring and turning the egg until all the uncooked parts become firm. Don't break up the egg, though. Try to keep the curds as large as possible. Transfer to a plate when the eggs are set but still moist and soft. Eggs are delicate, so they'll continue to cook for a few moments after they're on the plate.

"Little House" Maple Syrup Candy

2 cups real maple syrup

Using a candy thermometer, in a sturdy saucepan with high sides, bring the maple syrup to a boil. Turn the heat to very low and allow the syrup to continue boiling without stirring until the thermometer reads 233 degrees. Be careful that the syrup doesn't boil over - once maple syrup finally decides to boil, it really boils. When the reduced syrup has reached 233 degrees, remove it from the heat and allow to cool, still without stirring it, until the thermometer reads 110 degrees. Now it's time to beat the reduced syrup with a wooden spoon. Beat vigorously for several minutes. (It helps to sing when you do this.) You are making a transformation take place: As you beat, the syrup gradually turns a pale caramel color and it becomes stiff enough to hold a shape. Form into patties on a baking sheet and allow to cool completely.

My First Crush Was Not a Pop

I was eight years old the summer I had my first crush and it was a big one. He was an older man! Nineteen! He worked at the Pure Gas station at the bottom of the Cramer Road on Highway 61. My brother and I would jump on the black hose that led to a garage bell in the workshop. That would bring my sweetheart out front to pump gas for my mom. He would wash the windows and even check the oil, all for about 36 cents a gallon. He had the same name as my brother and I thought he hung the moon. He was cute, tan and had a beautiful smile. When he looked at me, sometimes I thought my heart would pound right out of my chest. My brother caught on and teased me about him all the time. Though I was only older by ten months, I thought my little brother was "such a child"….What did he know? After all this was the man I was going to marry (I just had to hurry up and grow up fast before he met someone else.)

Schroeder was a booming town back in 1971. There was Silvers Sawmill and Lumberyard, Cross River Café, Lamb's Grocery Store, Northland Hardware Store, a post office and no less than three gas stations: Shell Gas, Pure Gas and Skou's Garage. Each gas station also had a mechanics garage where the smell of grease and oil lingered in the air. Of course Lamb's Campground and Cabins were also in Schroeder at that time, just as they are today. It was quite an active community for a little "two blink town"… (Blink twice and you'd miss it as my Dad liked to say.) Over the years Schroeder has changed quite a bit. Today the gas stations are gone and you have to go to the Holiday station in Tofte if you want fuel. The gas costs a bit more now and you have to "pump it yourself." No cute teenager to wash your windows either….rats! Sadly, fires took both the hardware store and the café. Groceries were cheaper if you made a run to Duluth, and most people bought a washer and dryer to use at home; so there went the grocery store and the laundromat. All that is left from those days is the post office.

Whatever happened to my crush you ask? ....I remember VIVIDLY the day my brother decided to blab! (It was the exact same day I died of complete embarrassment!) Mr. Cutie-pants came up to the car, smiled at me through the open window and said "I heard you have a crush on me." My heart skipped a beat; I looked him straight in the eye and said "I have no idea what you're talking about". Then I rolled up the window. That certainly "crushed the crush". I decided older men were not for me and moved on to boys in my second grade class. My crush did marry the girl if HIS dreams and had a boatload of children. Ironically, I became their babysitter. The moral of the story? If you have a little brother with a big mouth, buy him lots of candy bars so he can't tell anyone you have a crush on them!

"That's why they call them crushes. If they were easy, they'd call them something else." ~ Sixteen Candles Quote

Almond Joy Chocolate Pie

Crust:
20 miniature Almond Joy candy bars or 10 large bars
¾ cups graham cracker crumbs

Filling:
½ cup granulated sugar
⅓ cup cornstarch
¼ cup Hershey's cocoa
¼ teaspoon salt
1 ½ half cups milk
1 teaspoon vanilla extract

16 miniature Almond Joy bars cut into one half-inch pieces (place candy in freezer 15 minutes for easy cutting)
Sweetened whipped cream or whipped topping

Preheat oven to 325 degrees. Lightly butter a nine-inch pie plate and set aside.

For the crust: Place crust ingredients in a food processor and process until mix is thoroughly blended. Press onto bottom and up the sides of pie plate. Bake 10 minutes. Remove and allow to cool completely.

For the filing: In a medium saucepan, stir together sugar, cornstarch, cocoa and salt. Blend in milk and cook over medium heat, stirring constantly with wire whisk until it boils, stirring for 1 minute. (This will be very thick.) Remove from heat and blend in vanilla and candy pieces and stir until melted.

Pour into pie crust and press plastic wrap onto surface. Refrigerate until set. Top with whipped cream when ready to serve.

Heath Bar Blizzard

1 Heath candy bar
¼ cup milk
2 ½ cups vanilla ice cream
1 teaspoon fudge topping

Freeze the Heath bar, and then break it into tiny pieces while still in the wrapper. Combine all ingredients in the blender and blend for 30 seconds on medium speed. Stop blender and stir mixture with a spoon, repeat until well mixed then pour into 16 ounce glass.

Frozen Milky Way Mousse

15 "Fun size" Milky Way Bars (or 36 miniatures or 5 regular size), divided
2 ½ cups heavy cream, divided
1 cup semisweet chocolate chips
1 teaspoon vanilla extract
Whipped cream for topping, optional

Chop candy bars, yielding about one cup. Combine with one half cup of the cream and chocolate chips in a large heatproof bowl over a pot of simmering water. Cook, stirring occasionally, until mixture is melted and combined. Set bowl aside to cool.

In another bowl combine vanilla extract with remaining 2 cups of cream; beat until stiff peaks form. Fold cream into chocolate mixture. Pour one half of mixture into a two quart freezer-proof bowl. Coarsely chop more candy bars, yielding about one third cup. Sprinkle over mousse. Top with remaining mousse. Freeze until firm, at least 6 hours or overnight.

Thaw slightly at room temperature before serving, about 10 minutes. Chop remaining candy bars, yielding about one third cup. Garnish with whipped cream and chopped candy.

My Dear Heart

Dear Heart. I like these words when used together. They sound friendly. I guess it makes sense then that I use them to describe one of my friends that I first met in kindergarten. Dear Heart uses the expression "Dearie" quite a bit when talking to me so I will make the great leap and believe that I am her Dear Heart too. We've kept in contact and had lunch just the other day. We laughed about grade school, high school, boyfriends, and girlfriends and of course each other. Even though we both live "in the cities" (anything south of Duluth is considered the Cities) we both still follow the North Shore News through the newspaper and of course through Facebook. (I am a big fan of Facebook's Flip Marais, he gives you a bird's eye view of Grand Marais.) The conversation somehow came around to psychology and child development. Dear Heart said that some people believe we have formed our personalities by the time we get to kindergarten. Hmm….That's an interesting theory but I'm not sure I believe it.

My Dear Heart and I were not always "Dearies". Especially not at first sight. We met at the arts and crafts table at the Birch Grove Elementary School kindergarten class. She and I do not agree on the details of this first meeting and all eye witnesses to the incident have either left the North Shore or pled the fifth. I recall Dear Heart sticking out her tongue at me in a very mean way for no reason at all then the teacher coming up behind her and pulled her beautiful blonde pony tail, scolding her that "Young ladies DO NOT stick out their tongues." (The hair pulling is a fact we both agree on as it is clear in our minds that we thought kindergarten teachers were supposed to be sweet and kind and play the piano while we all sang along….like Mary Poppins but without the flying…clearly our teacher had not seen the movie.)

Dear Heart remembers that I teased her about her terrible scissor cutting skills which then made her so mad she had stuck out her tongue to get back at me. She then claims I laughed out loud when the teacher pulled her hair. (The teasing part I dispute but come on, who wouldn't laugh at a good hair pulling? It's classic.)

Dear Heart and I eventually mended the fence and most likely formed an alliance against the teacher and her hair pulling ways... but the rest of the year is a blur. I do remember THE PARTY though. My birthday party came five weeks into the school year and I, of course, invited the ENTIRE CLASS. My parents were in the middle of putting on an addition and installing running water to the house at the time. More than twenty kids ran through the construction site dragging saw dust and scrap lumber here and there. My poor mother lost her voice in all the commotion but I made a huge haul in paper dolls. (Disney Paper Dolls and Barbie Paper Dolls were my favorite....I was not and am not a Raggedy Ann fan....I think she's kind of scary.)

So back to the kindergarten / personality theory..... If it is true that we have fully developed our personalities by kindergarten then it would seem I have always been a party loving girl with a sadistic sense of humor. Sounds about right!

"It is by chance we met. By choice we became friends." ~ Unknown

Delicious Mississippi Mud Cupcakes

1 cup chopped pecans
1 cup butter
4 ounces semisweet chocolate, chopped
2 cups sugar
1 ½ cups all-purpose flour
½ cup unsweetened cocoa
4 large eggs
1 teaspoon vanilla extract
1 teaspoon salt

1 (10.5 ounce) bag miniature marshmallows
One can Chocolate Frosting

Place pecans in a single layer on a baking sheet. Bake at 350 degrees for 8 to 10 minutes or until toasted. Microwave 1 cup butter and semisweet chocolate in a large microwave-safe glass bowl at HIGH 1 minute or until melted and smooth, stirring every 30 seconds. Whisk sugar and next 5 ingredients into chocolate mixture. Spoon batter evenly into 24 paper-lined muffin cups. Bake at 350 degrees for 20 minutes or until puffed. Sprinkle evenly with the miniature marshmallows, and bake 5 more minutes or until golden. Remove from oven and cool cupcakes in muffin pans 5 minutes. Remove cupcakes from pans, and place on wire rack. Microwave frosting until melty. Drizzle warm cakes evenly with chocolate frosting, and sprinkle with toasted pecans.

Sweet Potato Pecan Cupcakes

1 cup coarsely chopped pecans
2 cups sugar
1 cup butter, softened
4 large eggs
1 (16 ounce) can mashed sweet potatoes
⅔ cup orange juice
1 teaspoon vanilla extract
3 cups all-purpose flour
1 teaspoon baking powder
1 teaspoon ground cinnamon
½ teaspoon baking soda
½ teaspoon ground nutmeg
¼ teaspoon salt
One can Cream Cheese Frosting
Garnish: coarsely chopped pecans

Place pecans in a single layer in a shallow pan. Bake at 350 degrees for 8 to 10 minutes or until toasted, stirring once after 4 minutes. Beat sugar and butter at medium speed with an electric mixer until blended. Add eggs, 1 at a time, beating until blended after each addition. Whisk together mashed sweet potatoes, orange juice, and vanilla extract. Combine flour and next 5 ingredients. Add flour mixture to sugar mixture alternately with sweet potato mixture, beginning and ending with flour mixture. Beat at low speed just until blended after each addition. Fold in toasted pecans. Place foil baking cups in muffin pans, and coat with vegetable cooking spray; spoon batter into cups, filling two-thirds full. Bake at 350 degrees for 28 to 30 minutes or until a wooden pick inserted into center comes out clean. Remove immediately from pans, and cool 50 minutes to 1 hour or until completely cool. Spread cupcakes evenly with Cream Cheese Frosting. Garnish with more pecans.

Super Easy Lemonade Cupcakes

1 (6 ounce) can frozen lemonade concentrate, thawed
1 (18.25 ounce) package white cake mix
1 (8 ounce) carton sour cream
1 (3 ounce) package cream cheese, softened
3 large eggs
1 (12 ounce) can cream cheese frosting

Combine lemonade, cake mix, and next 3 ingredients in a mixing bowl. Beat at low speed with an electric mixer until moistened. Beat at high speed 3 minutes, stopping to scrape down sides. Spoon batter into 30 paper-lined muffin cups, filling each three-fourths full. Bake at 350 degrees for 22 minutes or until a wooden pick inserted in center comes out clean. Cool in pans on a wire rack 5 minutes. Remove cupcakes from pans; cool completely on wire rack. Spread evenly with frosting.

Everything you need to know about "The One"

My husband Mike and me at a wedding dance in 1996

My favorite brother-in-law proposed to his sweet girlfriend on St. Patrick's Day in Ely. (It wasn't a matter of green beer goggles. Apparently there are not many Irish in the town of Ely and my brother-in-law is quite German.) He planned the moment with a bottle of champagne on the shoreline and the perfect view of the lake. So romantic! I have been friends and roommates with Stephen for many, many years so I was very excited to see him so happy and comfortable with his decision to marry "the one." He just knew. I, on the other hand, had an lengthy evaluation process when I chose Michael.….three little words.….backpack through Europe. Seriously, if you are even considering marriage, plan a trip abroad and you will learn everything you need to know about "The One." Case and point:

One: Does he pack light? I'm not just talking about luggage. Is he a hoarder and collector of all your faults and mistakes? Does he save laundry list of every misstep you have ever made to bring up at parties of mixed company, or does he let it go, and consider your quirky traits be part of your charm? Light packers are much more fun on trips, especially the very long trip of marriage.

Two: Does he use a map? I feel if a man is willing to use the God given resources provided, such as, a map, to navigate his way through the streets of Paris, Amsterdam, Berlin, and Salzburg then he is the kind of guy who is willing to help guide his family through job changes, household moves, the education system, and the blessed healthcare bill. My friend, ignorance is not bliss, especially in a marriage.

Three: Is he willing to try new and foreign foods? This is a big one as I sometimes try new recipes that may lean toward the unusual. (Though I have toned it down a bit and removed the roasted garlic maker from the cupboard.) I still do not make fried chicken as well as his mothers, nor can I able to make his grandmother's famous graham cracker dessert, my husband is willing to try almost anything I make to stave off hunger and this, my friend, is a very lovable trait.

Four: Does he try to speak the language? Contrary to popular belief, not everyone in Europe speaks "some" English. Even those who do, it can be scattered and hard to understand, kind of like me when I am frazzled and trying to make a point. Is he willing to take the time, and sometimes use a translation dictionary, to fully understand the situation before throwing up his hands in frustration? Trust me you want someone who is willing to work to understand the complicated dialog we women sometimes use to make our point. To some men it all sounds like French.

And finally Five: Is he willing to share the load? Literally. When you find the perfect lead crystal bowls at a little shop in Prague does he offer to put a few in his backpack to help you avoid a hernia? (Knowing full well he will be carrying around an extra 20 pounds for the next three weeks and risking a detailed search at customs.) If so he, as a husband, will be willing to help unload the groceries, move furniture around the living room just because you need a change and sling hay bales to feed a horse he will never ride. He is truly the guy for me! Thank you Michael and welcome to the family, my new sister-in-law, Heather Holthaus!

> *"Choose your life's mate carefully. From this one decision will come 90 % of all your happiness or 90 % of your misery."* H. Jackson Brown, Jr.

These three macaroni and cheese recipes will get you through the first years of wedded bliss and beyond.

Mac and Cheese Bake

1 (16 ounce) package uncooked pasta shells
1 (10.75 ounce) can condensed cream of mushroom soup
1 (16 ounce) package shredded Cheddar cheese
4 ounces soda crackers, crushed

Preheat the oven to 350 degrees. Lightly grease a large casserole dish. Bring a large pot of lightly salted water to a boil. Stir in pasta and cook 12 minutes, or until tender but still firm. Drain, and transfer to a large bowl. Mix cream of mushroom soup, Cheddar cheese, with the pasta. Pour into the prepared casserole dish. Top with crushed crackers. Cover dish, and bake 30 minutes in the preheated oven. Remove cover, and continue baking 15 minutes, until cheese is bubbly and crackers are lightly browned.

Mac, Cheese and Peas

2 (10.75 ounce) cans Campbell's® Condensed Cheddar Cheese Soup
1 ½ cups milk
2 Tablespoons Dijon-style mustard
1 ½ cups frozen peas
3 cups elbow pasta, cooked and drained
¼ cup water
2 Tablespoons butter, melted
4 cups Corn Bread Stuffing

Stir the soup, milk, mustard, peas and pasta in a three quart shallow baking dish. Stir the water and butter in a large bowl. Add the stuffing and mix lightly to coat. Sprinkle the stuffing over the pasta mixture. Bake at 400 degrees for 30 minutes or until it's hot and bubbling.

Tuna Mac and Cheese

1 cup uncooked egg noodles
2 ½ cups sharp Cheddar cheese, shredded
¼ cup milk
¼ cup butter
⅓ cup cottage cheese
2 Tablespoons sour cream
1 (12 ounce) can tuna, drained

Bring a large pot of lightly salted water to a boil. Add pasta and cook for 8 to 10 minutes or until al dente; drain. In a saucepan over medium heat, combine cheddar cheese, milk, butter, cottage cheese, and sour cream; stir until melted. Pour cooked noodles into the cheese mixture and stir until well mixed. Stir in canned tuna; heat thoroughly.

Dimes from Heaven

Grandma Elsie Moe lived to be 104

My cousins Grandma Elsie died in on Monday, March 15th, 2009. (I give you the date for only one reason…in the two months since her death and I have received seventeen reminders that she looks down on me from heaven at least twice a week.) Born on October 23rd, 1905, she lived to be 104 years and five months. I've written about Grandma Elsie and her garden in the past. She loved to plant flowers and always had a beautiful vegetable garden. At one time my young son thought that her garden held the magic spell of youth because we always said "Grandma's garden keeps her young." She lived alone in her house after her husband Abner died in 1960. (If you do the math you realize she was widowed 17 years LONGER than she was married.) She begrudgingly moved to a nursing home when she was 103. Until then my cousin would catch her up on the ladder painting her window trim! She didn't want to bother anybody or ask for help.

I had never heard of dimes dropping from heaven until the day of Grandma's funeral. My sweet cousin was sweeping her kitchen floor, tidying up the house to put off her grief, when she turned around to find a brand new dime in the middle of the floor she had just cleaned. She held it up and said this is from Grandma. (I must admit I was a bit skeptical but it was her first smile of the day so I played along.) Well Grandma showed me; because later as I was getting out of the car, there was a dime on the ground right next to my foot! I picked it up and didn't say a word. Two days later I found a dime on the Holiday gas station sidewalk. Ok, ok this all might have been a coincidence but a dime in my shoe??? I tell you no lies; there was a dime in my shoe just a week later. Now they show up everywhere. In my pockets, under my desk, outside in the grass, at the park….My friend I am now a true believer! I swear to goodness, Dear Grandma Elsie is dropping dimes from heaven!

I am not sure why it is dimes that we find. My first thought is that it is because Grandma was a centenarian, and if you live more than 100 years you are given dimes to drop instead of mere pennies. It also could be that a dime is a sign of love tenfold. Think about it: if Grandma dropped a dime a week on each and every one of her 23 grandchildren; 48 great-grandchildren; and 18 great-great-grandchildren that would be 4628 dimes in this next year alone. (We could plant a city park full of flowers!) Whatever the reason, I am now saving these precious dimes in a jar and when I have enough I will plant a perennial flower in my garden in her memory. After all, if I plan to live to 104 I will need my garden to keep me young. My husband Mike can paint the trim on the house though, he'll only be 101!

"Heaven is under our feet as well as over our heads." ~ Henry David Thoreau

Grandma Elsie's Rhubarb Torte – From My sweet Cousin Dawn

Crust: 1 cup butter, 2 cups flour and 4 Tablespoons sugar. Mix well and press into a 9 by 13 pan. Bake 15 minutes at 350 degrees.

Filling: 6 cups rhubarb, cut into small pieces, 1 cup milk, 2 cups sugar, 6 egg yolks, and 4 Tablespoons flour. Mix well and pour over baked crust. Bake for 45 to 50 minutes at 350 degrees.

Topping: 6 egg whites and 2 Tablespoons sugar. Whip until stiff and soft peaks form. Spread over torte and bake 3 minutes at 450 degrees, (just until browned). Serve warm or cold. Delicious!

Rhubarb Upside Down Cake – from Rose Mary Nelson

1 Box white cake mix plus ingredients to prepare
½ pint whipping cream
3 cups rhubarb
1 ⅓ cups sugar
1 Tablespoon cinnamon

Make a white cake (per box or recipe directions), pour into a 9 by 13 pan. Mix together the rhubarb, sugar and cinnamon. Sprinkle over cake batter. Pour ½ pint whipping cream over rhubarb. Bake at 350 degrees for 50 minutes. Let stand 15 minutes, tip out onto a cake plate or serve from the pan.

Rhubarb Crumble – from Patty Klug

Place 3 cups diced rhubarb in a 9 by 13 pan.

Batter:
3 eggs
2 Tablespoons flour

1 ½ cup sugar

Pour this over rhubarb

Mix together until crumbly:
1 cup flour
½ cup brown sugar
1 teaspoon baking soda
⅓ cup butter

Sprinkle this on top of batter. Bake at 350 degrees for 45 minutes. Serve with whipped cream.

Treat Me Like A Child, Please

When I was in elementary school I had a love / hate relationship with the summer months. I loved that school was out; but I hated that I now couldn't see my friends every day; I loved the warm sunshine, camping, bonfires and s'mores; I hated the boredom, loneliness and being hot. To this day my parents do not have air conditioning of any kind, not even a window unit. My dad claims Lake Superior is the only air conditioner needed on the North Shore. I know we drove my mother crazy hanging around the house all day. We started to sound like a broken record repeating "There's nothing to do." She would say, go outside, take a nap or read a book! Finally, "Find something to do or I will find some chores for you to do!" I realize that I now sound exactly the same. But I also started thinking: how wise it would be if I listened to the advice I was giving my children.

Go Outside and Play. When was the last time I actually "played" outside? I don't mean weeding the garden, planting flower beds, feeding the animals or anything of the kind. I mean just play. I should just pick up a ball and throw it around. Or sit in the grass and build something out of sticks. Maybe even make an old fashioned mud pie. (Now that might be fun!)

Take a nap. Yes, please may I take a nap? Preferably in a hammock or the sky chair in the back yard. I fought naps tooth and nail when I was young. My mom would have us "rest" right after our lunch of grilled cheese and Campbell's soup. I could drag that meal on forever just to avoid giving in and taking a nap. Now I think I would actually pay for the chance at a nice afternoon nap.

Read a Book. In the 70's (Or the days of the dinosaurs as my children like to refer to my childhood) we obviously did not have laptops, Kindles, iPods or iPads. There was nothing better than curling up under a birch tree with a good book. This is the one order I took from my mom on a regular basis. I loved to read. In the summer the bookmobile would make a stop in Schroeder and I would start in the front and browse all the way to the back finding two or three books. I can honestly say this was and still is one of my favorite past times, though I just don't remember the last time someone actually told me to pick up a book and read. Now it's a guilty pleasure. I know that I, and several of my friends, try to squeeze in a chapter or two between laundry loads.

It's Bath Night! This was the worst! Sunday night was bath night. We had to try to get in, out, dried and dressed before Wild Kingdom and the Wonderful World of Disney. Until I was six we had no running water or indoor plumbing so it wasn't as easy as you might think. I now truly enjoy an evening when I have time for a long bath. The hotter the better.

So I tell my children, you can be the parent and I'll be the child. I will act on each piece of advice with great enthusiasm! I promise to be the best behaved child ever as I play, read, nap and bathe my way right through the summer months. Peace.

"It is a happy talent to know how to play." ~ *Ralph Waldo Emerson*

When summer is giving you lemons, make lemon pie, lemon bars or lemon cake!

Lemon Meringue Pie

1 cup white sugar
2 Tablespoons all-purpose flour
3 Tablespoons cornstarch
¼ teaspoon salt
1 ½ cups water
2 lemons, juiced and zested
2 Tablespoons butter

4 egg yolks, beaten
1 (9 inch) pie crust, baked
4 egg whites
6 Tablespoons white sugar

Preheat the oven to 350 degrees.

Lemon Filling: In a medium saucepan, whisk together 1 cup sugar, flour, cornstarch, and salt. Stir in water, lemon juice and lemon zest. Cook over medium-high heat, stirring frequently, until mixture comes to a boil. Stir in butter. Place egg yolks in a small bowl and gradually whisk in 1/2 cup of hot sugar mixture. Whisk egg yolk mixture back into remaining sugar mixture. Bring to a boil and continue to cook while stirring constantly until thick. Remove from heat. Pour filling into baked pastry shell.

Meringue: In a large glass or metal bowl, whip egg whites until foamy. Add sugar gradually, and continue to whip until stiff peaks form. Spread meringue over pie, sealing the edges at the crust.

Bake for 10 minutes, or until meringue is golden brown.

Lemon Bars

Crust:
1 cup all-purpose flour
⅓ cup butter, softened
¼ cup powdered sugar

Topping:
1 cup sugar
2 eggs
2 Tablespoons all-purpose flour

2 Tablespoons lemon juice
½ teaspoon lemon extract
½ teaspoon baking powder
¼ teaspoon salt
Powdered sugar for garnish

Combine the flour, butter and powdered sugar; pat into an eight-inch square baking pan. Bake at 375 degrees for 15 minutes.

Meanwhile, in a large mixing bowl, combine sugar, eggs, flour, lemon juice, extract, baking powder and salt in a mixing bowl. Mix until frothy; pour over crust. Bake for 18 to 22 minutes or until light golden brown. Dust with powdered sugar.

Lemon Cake

1 (18.25 ounce) package yellow cake mix
1 (3 ounce) package lemon flavored gelatin
¾ cup vegetable oil
4 eggs
¾ cup water
¼ teaspoon lemon extract
1 cup powdered sugar
4 Tablespoons lemon juice

Combine gelatin mix and cake mix. Mix well. Add next 4 ingredients - oil, eggs, water and lemon extract. Mix lightly. Bake according to instructions on back of cake box.

Frosting: Combine powdered sugar and lemon juice. When cake is done, and while still hot, ice with frosting.

Love at First Sight

Milton Kinny, Art Anderson, LaVonne (Allard) Anderson,
Bonnie (Allard) Moe and flower girl, Donna (Allard) Kruger
Robinson on my parents wedding day June 10th, 1961

How long does it take to fall in love?? Do you believe in love at first sight or does love grow over time? If so, just how much time is needed to decide if it is true love, or maybe a just a crush? Do you ever ask yourself how your life would be different if you stayed with your first high school sweetheart, married him and lived happily ever after? Let me tell you this, I am here today because my parent did just that.

Recently I visited the North Shore with my son Jack. We had a great time in Grand Marais, walking out along the break wall, eating Sven and Ole pizza and, of course, shopping at Ben Franklin. Just as we were about to leave my parents house in Schroeder on Sunday morning the doorbell rang and in walked a man I have not laid eyes on in 20 years or more. It is him I have to thank that I am here today. (No he did not save my life at any time during my wild childhood, but he did introduce my parents.) My dad lived in Onamia and my mother was a high school senior at Cook County High all set to graduate in 1961. This great friend convinced my dad to take a trip to the North Shore one weekend just to meet my mom. I believe it must have been love at first sight or at least within the first 72 hours because that's just how long it took them to fall in love and drive to Duluth to buy a marriage license.

The two of them thought they were pulling one over on my grandparents by buying the license in Duluth. (They thought if they bought it at the courthouse in Grand Marais someone would tell.) Little did they know the Duluth paper published all marriage license purchases in the paper each day. Mrs. Lamb called my Grandma pronto and let the cat out of the bag. Needless to say, my Grandparents were surprised! My mom was certain she had made the right choice and six days after she graduated from high school she walked down the aisle and married my dad. His friend stood right by his side as his "Best Man"...which I think is fitting. Their "love at first sight" still holds strong 49 years later. I am inspired. Love you Mom and Dad! Thanks Milton!

"We were given: Two hands to hold. To legs to walk. Two eyes to see. Two ears to listen. But why only one heart? Because the other was given to someone else. For us to find."

Summer Tomato Pie

1 (9 inch) deep dish pie crust
4 large tomatoes, peeled and sliced
½ cup chopped fresh basil

3 green onions, thinly sliced
½ pound bacon - cooked, drained, and chopped (optional, skip if vegetarian)
½ teaspoon garlic powder
1 teaspoon dried oregano
½ teaspoon crushed red pepper
2 cups shredded Cheddar cheese
¼ cup mayonnaise

Preheat oven to 375 degrees. In alternating layers, fill pastry shell with tomatoes, basil, scallions, bacon, garlic powder, oregano, and red pepper. In a small bowl, mix cheese with mayonnaise. Spread mixture over top of pie. Cover loosely with aluminum foil. Bake for 30 minutes. Remove foil from top of pie and bake an additional 30 minutes. Serve warm or cold.

Kiwi Salsa

I decided to try this recipe because I love kiwi and I love salsa. Delicious!

6 kiwis, peeled and diced
1 small onion, diced
1 jalapeno pepper, diced
2 Tablespoons lime juice
1 Tablespoon olive oil
1 teaspoon honey
½ teaspoon cumin
½ teaspoon curry powder

Mix kiwi, onion, jalapeno pepper, lime juice, olive oil, honey, cumin, and curry powder together in bowl. Cover and allow to rest for 1 hour at room temperature. Refrigerate until ready to serve.

Grilled Veggie Sandwich

¼ cup mayonnaise
3 cloves garlic, minced
1 Tablespoon lemon juice
⅛ cup olive oil
1 cup sliced red bell peppers
1 small zucchini, sliced (Yuck)
1 red onion, sliced
1 small yellow squash, sliced
2 (six-inch) Focaccia bread pieces split horizontally
½ cup crumbled feta cheese

In a bowl, mix the mayonnaise, minced garlic, and lemon juice. Set aside in the refrigerator. Preheat the grill for high heat. Brush vegetables with olive oil on each side. Brush grate with oil. Place bell peppers and zucchini closest to the middle of the grill, and set onion and squash pieces around them. Cook for about 3 minutes, turn, and cook for another 3 minutes. The peppers may take a bit longer. Remove from grill, and set aside. Spread some of the mayonnaise mixture on the cut sides of the bread, and sprinkle each one with feta cheese. Place on the grill cheese side up, and cover with lid for 2 to 3 minutes. This will warm the bread, and slightly melt the cheese. Watch carefully so the bottoms don't burn. Remove from grill, and layer with the vegetables. Enjoy as open faced grilled sandwiches.

Too Many Kitties!

My neighbor's sweet little boy came running into the house declaring Madam Marie "laid" more kittens! I said I help find them under the deck. As I lay laughing on the ground pulling out baby kitten after baby kitten from under her porch I remembered my favorite riddle, let's see if you can solve this...

The school bus driver picked up seven little girls, each of the seven little girls had seven pink backpacks. Each of the backpacks held seven cats and each of the seven cats had seven kittens. How many <u>legs</u> were on the bus when it arrived at the school???

Let's just say cats multiple fast! (This is Madam Marie's second litter of seven kittens this year.) Our family happily adopted two of the spring litter as our cat Spooky died last year at the ripe old age of sixteen. We only had her the last seven years of her life as she was a rescue, but you couldn't have asked for a nicer cat. She walked up our driveway in South Haven on the first day we moved in. We had to adopt her; she was coal black and it was only three weeks before Halloween. (We all know black cats don't fare well on Halloween night.)

My daughter Zoë's first kitten also came on Halloween when she was four. She dressed up like a witch and used an old basket for trick or treating at her Montessori School. One of the parents had brought a batch of kittens to the party (clever parents) and before we knew it she had a little gray boy in her basket as her treat! She named him Smokey, he was adorable and he LOVED Zoë. He would sleep with her and follow her everywhere. He even endured being dressed up in old baby outfits and pulled around in her wagon!

Oddly enough, I did not grow up loving cats. My Grandma

Isabelle had a number of cats and kittens but I didn't like any of them. They would hide under her wood stove in the kitchen and scratch my bare feet as I ran through the room. One night I awoke during a sleepover at Grandmas only to find a huge calico cat sitting on my chest. I screamed bloody murder because I thought she was waiting to claw my toes. Grandpa Haven was not happy! As it turned out that cat was just looking for a warm place to "lay" a new batch of kittens! If memory serves me correct – she had seven!

Did you figure out the answer to the riddle??? 10,992 legs if you include the bus driver! Now that my friend is a lot of legs!

"Women and cats will do as they please, and men and dogs should relax and get used to the idea."~ Robert A. Heinlein

Big Batch Meatballs

5 pounds ground beef (or ground turkey)
3 eggs
1 ½ cups quick cooking oatmeal
2 large onions, diced
1 Tablespoon salt
1 Tablespoon pepper

Italian Meatball Option:
Meat can be divided and these additional seasoning added to half batch for variation.

1 Tablespoon dried basil
1 teaspoon crushed red pepper
1 teaspoon garlic powder
1 teaspoon dried oregano
⅓ cup Parmesan cheese

Preheat oven to 400 degrees. Place beef in large bowl. Measure remaining ingredients in blender. Pour blender contents over beef and mix well using hands if necessary. Shape into one inch balls and place on cookie sheets. Bake for 20 minutes. Pour off any fat and cool for 30 minutes. While still on tray freeze solid (usually overnight). Pack loosely in food safe freezer bags. Label and date. Use as needed. Can be added to sauces frozen and simmered until heated through.

Big Batch Butterscotch Cookies

1 ½ cups butter, softened
3 cups packed brown sugar
3 eggs
1 Tablespoon vanilla extract
5 cups all-purpose flour
1 Tablespoon baking powder
1 ½ teaspoons baking soda
½ teaspoon cream of tartar

In a large mixing bowl, cream the butter and brown sugar. Add eggs, one at a time, beating well after each addition. Beat in vanilla. Transfer to a larger bowl if necessary. Combine flour, baking powder, baking soda and cream of tartar; gradually add to the creamed mixture. Drop by level Tablespoonfuls 2 inches apart onto ungreased baking sheets. Bake at 350 degrees for 10 to 12 minutes or until golden brown. Remove to wire racks to cool. Makes 10 dozen cookies.

Big Batch Vegetable Soup

2 Tablespoons olive oil
2 cups chopped onions or thinly sliced leeks (whites only)
1 cup thinly sliced celery
2 teaspoons Italian seasoning
Coarse salt and ground pepper

3 cans (14.5 ounces each) vegetable or chicken broth
1 can (28 ounces) diced tomatoes, with juice
1 Tablespoon tomato paste
8 cups mixed fresh or frozen vegetables, such as carrots, corn, green beans, lima beans, peas, potatoes, and zucchini (Yuck!). Cut the larger vegetables into smaller pieces to reduce the cooking time.

Heat oil in a large stockpot over medium heat. Add onions or leeks, celery, and Italian seasoning; season with salt and pepper. Cook, stirring frequently, until onions are translucent, 5 to 8 minutes. Add broth, tomatoes and their juice, tomato paste, and 3 cups water to pot; bring mixture to a boil. Reduce heat to a simmer, and cook, uncovered, 20 minutes. Add vegetables to pot, and return to a simmer. Cook, uncovered, until vegetables are tender, 20 to 25 minutes. Season with salt and pepper, as desired. Let cool before storing. This freezes well.

Need a Weapon?

If said I was going to just give you something that weighted ninety three pound <u>for free</u> what would guess it might be???

  A) A week's worth of washing.
  B) An average size middle school student.
  C) A car load of zucchini and a cookbook.

I happen to have A and B in my home as we speak but I would seriously pass on to you C in a heartbeat if it were to fall at my doorstep because I do in fact have the cookbook "What to do with 93 pounds of Zucchini or aptly named Zucchini Cookery." Fate laid this book in my hands last week at the St. Ignatius Church Rummage sale. I was digging through the books and there it was at the bottom of a box...I almost dropped it like a snake then I thought "Sandy, don't be silly, there might be something to this zucchini craze after all." The cover reads that if I were to make each and every recipe in the book I would have ridden the world of 93 pounds of zucchini. (Yeah!)

I spent the next several hours reading this interesting booklet. The recipe that stood out the most is for one of my favorite foods, Lasagna. This monster dish calls for three full pounds of zucchini! Along with all the beautiful cheese and expensive ground beef I am sure I would be that last person on earth to try to "thinly slice a huge zucchini" to replace delicious lasagna noodles. Or my second choice Armenian Casserole that calls for only one pound of zucchini. (This tells me that they grow way too many zucchini in Armenia too!) And the worst of the worst, let's use our personal time, energy and electricity to <u>dry</u> zucchini to use for "snacking chips"??? Please, not when I can use my valuable time to dry grapes and make my own raisins!

Now there is a lady in Frenchtown, Montana who I feel has the right idea. When she was bit in the leg by a 200 pound black bear she reached for the most threatening weapon she could find. I might have reached for a knife or a mallet but she smacked him right across the nose with a six pound zucchini!! You might argue I should grow one in my garden for just such a purpose, but I must remind you in addition to a six pound weapon we all know I'd end up with 93 pounds of zucchini to contend with!

"If life hands you lemons make lemonade, if life hands you tomatoes make Bloody Mary's and if life hands you zucchini, smack a bear with it!" ~ *The ever wise, Sandy Holthaus*

Recipes that tastes delicious WITHOUT zucchini:

Chocolate Pudding Fudge Cake

1 (18.25 ounce) package devil's food cake mix
1 (3.9 ounce) package instant chocolate pudding mix
1 cup sour cream
1 cup milk
½ cup vegetable oil
½ cup water
4 eggs
2 cups semisweet chocolate chips
6 Tablespoons butter
1 cup semisweet chocolate chips

Preheat oven to 350 degrees. Grease and flour a 10 inch Bundt pan. In a large bowl, combine cake mix, pudding mix, sour cream, milk, oil, water and eggs. Beat for 4 minutes, and then mix in 2 cups chocolate chips. Pour batter into prepared pan. Bake 40 to 50 minutes, or until a toothpick inserted into the center of the cake comes out clean. Cool 10 minutes in the pan, then turn out onto a wire rack and cool completely.

To make the Glaze: Melt the butter and 1 cup chocolate chips in a double boiler or microwave oven. Stir until smooth and drizzle over cake.

Chocolate Pear Spice Cake

3 eggs
1 ⅓ cups applesauce
3 Tablespoons molasses
½ cup butter, melted
1 (18.5 ounce) package yellow cake mix
2 teaspoons ground cinnamon
1 teaspoon ground nutmeg
¼ teaspoon ground cloves
1 Tablespoon finely shredded orange peel
1 small pear, peeled and thinly sliced
½ cup pecans, chopped
1 (2.6 ounce) bar milk chocolate, coarsely chopped

Preheat an oven to 350 degrees. Grease and flour a 10 inch spring form pan. Use an electric mixer to beat the eggs, applesauce, molasses, and butter in a large bowl. Beat in the cake mix along with the cinnamon, nutmeg, cloves, and orange peel. Mix on medium speed for 4 minutes. Pour batter into prepared pan. Top the unbaked cake with pear slices; sprinkle evenly with the pecans and chopped chocolate. Bake until a toothpick inserted in the center comes out clean, about 55 to 60 minutes. Cool for 25 minutes before removing from pan.

Banana Bundt Cake

2 Tablespoons lemon juice
⅔ cup milk
2 large very ripe bananas, mashed
1 (18.25 ounce) package butter cake mix
1 teaspoon baking soda
½ cup butter, softened
3 eggs
1 teaspoon vanilla extract

Preheat oven to 350 degrees. Grease and flour a Bundt pan. Put 1 Tablespoon lemon juice in a measuring cup with ⅔ cup milk. Set aside. Mash bananas with a fork, adding the remaining 1 Tablespoon lemon juice to them as you mash. Set aside.

In a large bowl, combine cake mix and baking soda. Stir to combine. Add bananas, softened butter, milk mixture, eggs and vanilla. Beat at low speed until moistened (about 30 seconds). Beat at medium speed for 4 minutes. Pour into prepared pan.

Bake for 30 to 35 minutes, or until center of cake springs back when lightly tapped. A toothpick stuck in the center may leave a slight crumb. Allow to cool on a wire rack.

Put the Big Rocks First

I am sure many of you have heard the analogy about putting the big rock first. If not, here is a brief recap of the story: An instructor was lecturing his students and at one point, he said, "Okay, time for a quiz." He reached under the table and pulled out a wide-mouthed gallon jar. He then filled the jar with big rocks. Then he asked, "Is this jar full?" Everyone said, "Yes." He then reached under the table and pulled out a bucket of gravel. Then he dumped some gravel in and shook the jar and the gravel went in all the little spaces left by the big rocks. Then he grinned and said once more, "Is the jar full?" By this time the class was on to him. "Probably not," they said. He then brought out a bucket of sand. He started dumping the sand and it went into all of the little spaces left by the rocks and the gravel. Once more he looked up and said, "Now is this jar full?" Yes? He then grabbed a pitcher of water and began to pour it in. He got about a quart of water in that jar. Then he said, "Well, what's the point?" Somebody said, "Well, there are gaps, and if you work really hard you can always fit some more things into your life."

"No," he said, "that's not the point. The point is this: If you hadn't put the big rocks in first, you never would have fit them in. Now you need to decide what your big rocks are."

Two weeks ago I took the kids to the North Shore to visit my parents. We love going down to the beach. There we either throw rocks into the lake or pick up favorite colors or shapes. I am known to love heart shaped rocks and there is one beach in particular where it seems I always find one or two. This time I found five heart shaped rocks in a variety of colors. I built them into a rock cairn. (Though I cheated and used glue....rock cairns are beautiful but hard to balance.) **Note: Spending time on the shore with my children and parents, BIG ROCK.**

We visited Sven and Ole's for a pizza and in the process ran into two 1982 graduates Carl and Julie. One with his beautiful family sharing the North Shore with his kids and one a brand new Grandmother! (Yikes, where did the time go and please Lord don't make me a Grandma for another 10 years or so!) **Note: Introducing my kids to people who knew me back when I thought I knew it all! BIG ROCK.**

My parents like to be with family and friends and my kids have a good time with them. Usually this means several games of cards or dominos instead of watching TV. My youngest son's greatest joy came this weekend when he played a perfect game of Up and Down the River and for the very first time EVER beat my dad. (If you have had the chance to play cards with my dad you know you rarely win! He's very good.) **Note: Playing cards with Grandma and Grandpa just like I did as a kid, though I never beat my dad, BIG ROCK.**

We couldn't get Grandpa and Grandma to go down the Alpine Slide (something about a fear of stopping) but Grandma did hold the towels while all the kids stripped down to their skivvies and plunge into the lake up to their knees. (I should mention here that it was 42 degrees outside.) The original plan was to jump in the lake but the waves were quite high and I was worried someone might get pulled under, and let's face it I was not going in after them! **Note: Scaring Grandma half to death but making a lifetime memory, BIG ROCK.**

My parents, my kids, my husband, family and friends are my big rocks. I have spent a lot of time trying to put them into my jar first but then I realized there is another rock I need to get in there before all the gravel, sand and water fill up the jar; that's me. For my rock in the jar I will find the perfect heart shaped rock and place it right on top!

"Action expresses priorities." ~ *Mahatma Gandhi*

It's Hot Dish Season! (A home cooked meal
for the entire family. BIG ROCK.)

Double Tater Tot Cheese Hotdish

2 pounds (browned) ground beef
1 (12 ounce) can peas, drained
1 (12 ounce) can corn, drained
1 (12 ounce) can cream of corn
12 ounces of Velveeta or 12 American cheese singles
1 cup milk
2 (10 ¾ ounce) cans cream of mushroom soup
2 (24 ounce) package tater tots
1 medium onion, optional

Substitute: Frozen vegetables can be used, but require one half
hour longer baking time. Different canned vegetables can be
used also.

Preheat oven to 350 degrees. Brown ground beef with finely
chopped onion in a medium frying pan. Then in a medium
saucepan, on medium heat, melt the Kraft singles with the milk,
then add the cream of mushroom to make a thick sauce. Next, in
a 4 quart casserole dish, mix ground beef mixture with vegetables
and 1 package of tater tots. Pour cheese sauce over mixture and
mix with spoon. Add the other package of tater tots to the top.
Leave uncovered and bake for 1 hour.

Shepherd's Pie

2 Tablespoons olive oil
1 medium yellow onion, chopped
3 stalks celery, thinly sliced
2 pounds of ground turkey
¼ cup flour

1 teaspoon salt
1 teaspoon pepper
½ teaspoon thyme
3 cups low sodium chicken broth
1 (16 ounce) package of frozen mixed veggies
1 (28 ounce) package of frozen mashed potatoes or left over homemade
½ cup grated Parmesan cheese

Preheat the oven to 400 degrees. Prepare entire bag of mashed potatoes according to package directions. If necessary, thin the potatoes a bit with some milk. They should be wet, but thick. Set aside. Meanwhile, heat oil in a large skillet over medium heat. Add onion and celery and cook until they begin to soften, about 5 minutes. Add turkey and break apart with a spatula. Cook turkey until no longer pink. Sprinkle flour, salt, pepper and thyme over the turkey and stir to combine. Stir in chicken broth, raise heat to high and bring to a boil. Stir in package of frozen veggies and simmer for 5 minutes more. Remove from heat. Pour turkey and vegetable mixture into a 9 by 13 casserole dish that has been sprayed with cooking spray. Spoon little piles of mashed potatoes over the top and smooth out with a spatula. If desired, fluff them up with the tines of a fork for better browning. Sprinkle the Parmesan cheese over the top and bake for 30 minutes, or until golden brown and bubbling.

Swiss Chicken Bake

6 chicken breasts
6 slices Swiss cheese
1 can cream of mushroom soup
¼ cup milk
2 cups stuffing mix
½ cup butter, melted

Lay chicken breasts in slow cooker. Top with cheese. Combine soup and milk and spoon over cheese. Sprinkle stuffing mix on top. Drizzle melted butter over stuffing mix. Cover; Cook on low 8 to 10 hours or high 3 to 4 hours.

Ten Things I Hate About Winter

If you hate the winter cold STOP READING THIS COLUMN! It won't help because I am about to whine a blue streak and you might have to lie down to recoup after you read this.

Number One – I went outside this morning with SLIGHTLY damp hair only to find icicles in my pony tail when I was at the grocery store. Hair icicles! Tell that to someone who grew up in Miami. They won't believe you.

Number Two – Frozen stock tanks. I had to bust through two inches of ice to give the alpacas a drink. (I know I should have had the heater on sooner but I wanted to save on the electric bill.) **Number two and a half**: The water hose was frozen solid so I had to hang it in the tub to thaw. AAARRRGGG and YUCK at the same time!

Number Three – Bedtime at 5:00? I am an early riser. I always have been but that means I have an internal clock that believes if it is light out I should be up and if it is dark outside I should be tucked into bed. I now sleep 15 hours a day. (Not really but my body wants to that's for sure.) Hint: November through March - Don't call after 8:30…seriously… I'm asleep.

Number Four – Yes you can freeze your fingers to the water hydrant and it doesn't have to be much below 32 degrees to do so. I try to remember to wear gloves but when I'm in a hurry…. Ever watched a Christmas Story? I cringe at the flagpole scene every time.

Number Five – Scraping frosty car windows! I am short and reaching the middle without getting my jacket all dirty from the side of the van is next to impossible. I will admit, but don't tell anyone, I try to skip the scraping part and go straight to using a half gallon of window washer to clear the windshield in the morning. I use more fluid in the winter than any other time of year.

Number Six – I eat too much when it's cold. I don't know why, salads just don't cut it when there's snow on the ground. Thick soups, homemade bread, warm apple pie (at least its fruit) and buttery popcorn are my winter favorites. Minnesota fashion also makes it just a little too easy to cover up that extra five pounds I find just waiting for me in the spring. (Who am I kidding? We all know it's an extra ten!)

Number Seven – I hate winter driving! I am a tense, white knuckle winter driver and I will be the first to admit it. I just want to stay on the road and not have anyone hit me either. It doesn't help if someone else drives I am just as nervous with them behind the wheel. It's best if I fall asleep. That way I don't grip the chicken handle and have my feet on the dash the whole time! No child needs to see that.

Number Eight – Hunting season! I am not upset about the hunting of deer as I understand that without hunting we would be overrun by these animals but seriously do you have to start blasting your guns at the first crack of dawn and continue shooting until dusk??? I thought most hunters could kill on the first shot but this must be a myth because I hear at least four rounds in a row… it's Bambi for goodness sake not an elephant.

Number Nine – Runny noses! Nuff said!

Number Ten – It lasts too darn long! Five months is just too much. Don't try to tell me it's only four months either. Winter for me begins November 1st and doesn't end until April 1st. That, my friend is five full months and I choose to forget those years when it has snowed mid October and we've had freezing rain in April. (I have seasonal amnesia.)

Thank you for listening to my whining and complaining. If you have the good fortune to be reading this from the warmth of Arizona, Florida or any place other than South Haven, Minnesota, please send me a postcard with a little sunshine. I think I'm going to need it!

Winter is nature's way of saying, "Up yours." ~Robert Byrne

Winter Warm up Drinks!

Honey Bee Tea for One

1 Cinnamon tea bag
1 ½ cups skim milk
1 Tablespoon honey
A dash of vanilla

Heat the milk, honey and vanilla in a saucepan. Pour over tea bag and let it seep. Drink immediately!

Tea and Cider Wassail

6 cups freshly brewed hot tea (I use Lipton regular tea)
6 cups cranberry juice
6 cups apple cider or apple juice
3 cups orange juice
1 ½ cups sugar
1 ¼ cups lemon juice
9 inches stick cinnamon, broken
¾ teaspoon whole cloves
Apple slices (optional)

In a six to eight quart Dutch oven, combine tea, cranberry juice, apple cider, orange juice, sugar, and lemon juice. For spice bag, place cinnamon and cloves in the center of a double thick, six-inch square of 100 percent cotton cheesecloth. Bring the corners of the cheesecloth together and tie with clean string. Add spice bag to juice mixture. Bring mixture to boiling, stirring with a wooden spoon to dissolve sugar; reduce heat. Cover and simmer for 30 minutes. Remove and discard spice bag. To serve, ladle the wassail into a heatproof punch bowl. If desired, garnish with apple slices. Makes about 22 (8 ounce) servings.

Slow cooker directions: Combine all the ingredients in a six quart slow cooker. Cover and cook on low heat setting for 5 to 6 hours or on high heat setting for 2 1/2 to 3 hours. Remove and discard spice bag. Keep warm on low heat setting for up to 2 hours.

Sweet Hot Buttered Rum (Easy Crockpot Recipe)

2 cups firmly packed brown sugar
½ cup butter
1 pinch salt
3 sticks cinnamon
4 whole cloves
½ teaspoon ground nutmeg
2 quarts hot water

2 cups rum
Whipped cream
Ground nutmeg

Put the first seven ingredients into a large crock pot. Add 2 quarts hot water. Stir well. Cover; cook on low for 5 hours. Stir in rum. Top individual servings with whipped cream and a dash of nutmeg.

A Trip Behind the Woodshed

I received and e-mail last week from a friend who was threatening to take her son behind the woodshed. I really did laugh out loud as I had not heard that expression in some time. (The last time was probably on an old Andy Griffith episode.) I asked my son Jack if he knew what it meant and surprisingly he did, although he personally has never even seen a woodshed let alone the back of a woodshed! (My current parenting tools do not involve a shed or wood of any kind, but hey, it's still early in the game.) I could not tell you about any personal woodshed trips. My dad would make these really chincy paddles out of cheap paneling. If we were naughty he would smack the paddle on the dining room table in a threatening way and I would burst into tears as the pieces flew. He never needed to actually hit me with it; it was enough just to hear that crack! I would straighten up and fly right (for the next few days anyway.) I tell my children I would probably start crying right now if I ever heard that sound again.

My great-grandma was a big believer in smacking children. Her philosophy was "Hit them as they walk by because they're either coming from it or heading to it!" I'm not sure what she thought "it" was but she was sure "it" was naughty. We laugh now but I was a little scared of her most of my young life. My grandma Isabelle, on the other hand only spanked me once that I remember and I have to admit I deserved it. I was playing with matches when I was supposed to be napping and I accidently lit the bedroom curtains on fire! I told her I just woke up and the room was burning. She didn't believe me. I ended up with a blistered bottom and blistered fingers but I never touched matches again! To this day I don't like paper match books. I guess some lessons last forever when driven home with a swat!

I was just thinking, why was it "behind" the woodshed? Didn't most people have outhouses? It seems to me the outhouse would have been an easier meeting place. It might be small, dark and not as sweet smelling as the woodshed but all the more reason to get in and get out in a hurry. (Or better yet not do anything to get sent there in the first place.) Today what would we use in place of the woodshed? Meet me at the side of the garage or out behind the fish house just doesn't have the same ring to it. Maybe I'll have my dad make me a supply of chincy paddles and I'll crack them on the table, though I run the risk of scaring myself more than the kids.

> *"The difference between a pat on the back and a kick in the pants is about three feet."* ~ *Unknown*

I just learned to cook on cedar planks. (A better use for wood then switches.) You can buy these in cooking shops, on the internet or make your own using UNTREATED cedar planks you might find in your woodshed. Remember to soak the planks thoroughly. These recipes are for <u>oven</u> plank cooking.

BBQ Plank Roast Pork

Some simple preparation in this barbecue plank roast pork recipe and your reward will be a BBQ sauce to die for.

3 pounds boneless pork roast
2 Tablespoons freshly ground black pepper
3 garlic cloves sliced into pegs
1 Tablespoon salt

For the sauce:
3.5 fl oz white wine
3 teaspoons corn starch mixed in water
A pinch of salt

Mix the salt and black pepper, make incisions in the pork and insert a garlic peg and a sprinkle of the salt and pepper combination. When all the garlic is used up, sprinkle the rest of the salt and pepper over the roast and you're ready to go. Place the pork on a preheated plank and cook for 1 hr 20 minutes at 350 degrees taking care to catch all the juices from the hollow in the plank (or that drip off) in a tray.

For the sauce, pour the juices in a saucepan together with the white wine and corn flour mix and gently bring to a boil stirring all the time. Taste the sauce and add the pinch of salt if you think necessary, likewise add a little more of the corn flour mix if you prefer a thicker sauce. Pour the sauce over the sliced pork, serve immediately and don't forget that there's a bottle of wine that needs finishing!

Roasted Cedar Plank Salmon

2 pounds of salmon fillet
3 Tablespoons vegetable oil
1 ½ Tablespoons soy sauce
1 ½ teaspoons chopped garlic
½ teaspoon salt
¼ teaspoon white pepper
⅓ cup Rye or Scotch Whiskey
1 Tablespoon brown sugar

Place salmon filet in a long shallow dish. Mix together all ingredients and pour over the salmon filet. Marinate for 30 minutes. Preheat oven to 400 degrees. Place the cedar plank directly on the oven rack and bake for 8 to 10 minutes. This will lightly toast the wood. Remove the plank from the oven and rub with a thin coating of olive oil while plank is still hot. Place salmon directly on the hot plank and roast on the plank for about ten minutes.

Cedar Planked Lemon Thyme Chicken

1 whole, (prefer organic) chicken, rinsed inside and out
1 large bunch of fresh lemon thyme
1 Tablespoon Sea salt
1 Tablespoon butter, softened
2 bulbs of garlic
Cedar plank, soaked in water for 20 minutes prior to use

Preheat your oven to 450 degrees. Set an oven rack in the middle. Place your cedar plank in an oven tray, place on the rack and let heat up till it starts to crackle. In the meantime, make a fragrant salt by pounding a large handful of lemon thyme with 1 to 2 Tablespoons of sea salt, till a rough paste is formed. Mix half of this paste with 1 Tablespoon of butter and reserve the other half.

Gently separate the skin above the breast from the flesh, so it doesn't tear and rub some lemon thyme butter underneath. Rub the remainder of the lemon thyme butter inside the cavity of the chicken, and then stuff it with some stalks of lemon thyme and garlic cloves. Secure the opening with a toothpick or truss it up. Rub the reserved lemon thyme paste on the outside of the chicken, ensuring all bits are well rubbed.

By this time, the cedar plank should be crackling. Bring it out of the oven and using a tea towel soaked in olive oil, rub it all over. Place the chicken on top of the plank, breast side up and pop in the oven. If at any time, you're worried the plank is getting too dry, put some water in the tray. Cook about one hour, plus 15 minutes for each pound or until juices run clear. (Example: 2 pound chicken would be 1 hour 30 minutes.) About 10 minutes before the end of the cooking time, flip the bird over so the underside crisps up. Once ready, bring out of the oven and leave to rest for 10 minutes.

What Exactly is a "Salty Dog"?

I happen to love salt and Lord knows I have met my share of dogs. (Both the two and four legged variety.) But how did the two ever get put together as an expression? I will tell you how – it is THE MOST delicious candy bar you will ever taste! Sea Salt and Dark Chocolate together is truly delightful! Delightful is not an expression I normally use but seriously I can find no better description to this delicious combination. For those who know me well I am a DIEHARD peanut butter / chocolate fan. (In fact my sons are lucky they are not named Reese.) But I am willing to step away from the peanut butter cup in favor of the Salty Dog.

Some of you will cringe but I ate lots of rock salt as a child. My dad would keep a large bag in the garage for making homemade ice cream. I would dig down to find the biggest piece and suck on it all afternoon like candy. Sometimes I liked to pretend the rocks were real diamonds and I was rich with a pocket full of gems. Later when I worked as a waitress at Satellites Country Inn I would fill a plate with hamburger pickles and salt them for my favorite afternoon snack. Salt was everywhere and easily attainable. It tasted soo good I never worried it could hurt me or cause health problems later in life. I can make a long list of salt laden foods I love…..green olives, sunflower seeds, capers, pretzels in honey mustard dip….and of course hot buttered popcorn with sea salt. (Have you tried topping your bag of popcorn with a bag of dark chocolate M & M's? Truly to die for.

I don't know why it took me so long to find the Salty Dog. Now that I have I think about it all the time. I bought a large bar and kept it in the freezer trying to just have one, or two, or three squares a day, finally I finished it and now I just enjoy buying it one piece at a time every few weeks, like a great reward for skipping the peanut butter cups at the grocery store. I tried to find a recipe so we could make our own "Salty Dog Chocolate Bar" but the best I could do was a drink made with gin and grapefruit juice. Until a recipe can be found we will have to purchase these "yummy Salty Dogs" from our favorite neighborhood chocolatier.

"A wise woman puts a grain of sugar into everything she says to a man, and takes a grain of salt with everything he says to her." ~ Helen Rowland

I thought you might enjoy some <u>low salt</u> appetizer options. These are really delicious!

<u>Apricot Chicken Wings</u>

2 pounds chicken wings
1 cup apricot preserves
2 Tablespoons cider vinegar
2 teaspoons hot pepper sauce
1 teaspoon chili powder
1 garlic clove, minced

Cut chicken wings into three sections; discard wing tips. In a small bowl, combine the remaining ingredients; pour one cup marinate into a large resealable plastic bag; add chicken. Seal bag and turn to coat. Refrigerate for 4 hours or overnight. Cover and refrigerate remaining marinade. Drain and discard marinade. Place wings in a greased foil lined 15 by 10 by 1 inch baking pan. Bake at 400 degrees for 30 to 35 minutes or until juices run clear, turning and basting occasionally with remaining marinade.

Low Sodium Guacamole

This mixture is also a great dressing for mixed green salads and is a good topping for fish or chicken.

½ cup fat-free sour cream
2 teaspoons chopped onion
⅛ teaspoon hot sauce
1 ripe avocado, peeled, pitted and mashed

In a small bowl, combine the sour cream, onion, hot sauce and avocado. Mix to blend the ingredients evenly. Serve with baked tortilla chips or sliced vegetables.

Low Salt Potato Skins

2 medium russet potatoes
Butter-flavored cooking spray
1 Tablespoon minced fresh rosemary
⅛ teaspoon freshly ground black pepper

Preheat the oven to 375 degrees. Wash the potatoes and pierce with a fork. Place in the oven and bake until the skins are crisp, about 1 hour. Carefully — potatoes will be very hot — cut the potatoes in half and scoop out the pulp, leaving about one eighth inch of the potato flesh attached to the skin. Save the pulp for mashed potatoes made later. Spray the inside of each potato skin with butter-flavored cooking spray. Press in the rosemary and pepper. Return the skins to the oven for 5 to 10 minutes. Serve immediately.

Are You Fun To Live With?

I once worked with a woman that had a no-nonsense personality. She wasn't rude per se, she just liked to keep it all business and no chit chat. A real hard nut to crack. At one point our company was entertaining clients from out of town and decided to take them to the play "How to Talk Minnesotan." It was hilarious "don't-cha-know" and much to my surprise "Miss All Business" had a huge part in the play! She was really funny and talented. Our clients commented that "Boy she must be a REAL HOOT to work with!" ("Um – no not really…" I thought but of course did not share.) I am aware that there is a time and a place for cutting loose but does the extreme have to be business crabby by day to comedian by night? Why was it more important for her to be funny for complete strangers than it would be for the people she worked with day after day after day??? What was she like at home with her family??

This point stuck with me…are we fun to live with?

How many times are we polite to our co-workers, neighbors and "other people's children" only to snip at our husband and kids for the smallest irritation? (Ahem, I am not necessarily talking about me….) But what would happen in our homes if we extended the same politeness to our families that we do to the mailman or our hair dresser? "Please" and "thank you" and "I appreciate that" would be part of the everyday norm. If we had to take a "text" or phone call while out having coffee with our spouse we would acknowledge it and apologize or say excuse me and not leave the other person hanging, feeling dumb. (I actually knew a woman whose husband brought a book to read when they ate out at restaurants….seriously not a guy I would find fun to live with!)

Having fun doesn't have to take lots of time or energy. Greet your family when they come home with a smile. Send them off with a 10 second kiss or a 5 second hug! (Sounds short but try kissing the back your hand for a full 10 seconds....it takes awhile.) Sign up for a joke of the day e-mail and share it over dinner. Offer to get a water or coffee if you're getting something for yourself. Learn a couple of card tricks or keep dice in your purse for those times when you have to wait at a doctor's office or restaurant. Ask your family to share three things about their day. (I do this with my kids when I pick them up from school and it leads to lots of interesting stories.) Use your imagination and remember to treat your family like you would a good friend...be fun to live with!

"Be who you are and say what you feel because those who mind don't matter and those who matter don't mind." ~ Dr. Suess

Creamy Pesto Shrimp Linguine

1 pound linguine pasta, cooked and drained
½ cup butter
2 cups heavy whipping cream
½ teaspoon ground black pepper
1 cup grate Parmesan cheese
⅓ cup pesto
1 pound large shrimp - peeled and deveined

In large skillet, melt the butter over medium heat; stir in the cream and pepper. Cook, stirring constantly, for 6 to 8 minutes or until hot. Add the grated parmesan cheese, stirring until thoroughly mixed. Stir in the pesto sauce and cook for 3 to 5 minutes, until thickened. Add the shrimp and cook until they turn pink, about 5 minutes. Serve over hot linguine.

Chicken Parmigiana

2 skinless, boneless chicken breast halves
2 ounces dried bread crumbs
1 egg, beaten
One (16 ounce) jar spaghetti sauce
2 ounces shredded mozzarella cheese
¼ cup grated Parmesan cheese

Preheat oven to 350 degrees. Dip chicken into beaten egg, then into the bread crumbs. Place chicken on a lightly greased cookie sheet and bake for 40 minutes. Pour half of the spaghetti sauce into a 9 by 13 baking dish. Add the chicken and top with the remaining sauce. Sprinkle mozzarella and Parmesan cheeses on top and bake in the oven for 20 minutes.

<u>Vegetarian Chili</u>

1 (28 ounce) can <u>tomatoes</u>, undrained
1 (16 ounce) jar chunky Salsa
1 (15 ounce) can black beans, rinsed, drained
1 (10 ounce) package frozen whole kernel corn
1 cup halved zucchini slices (Totally optional, in fact I would prefer you skip!)
1 teaspoon chili powder
1 (8 ounce) package shredded cheddar <u>cheese</u>

Mix tomatoes, salsa, beans, corn, zucchini and chili powder in saucepan. Bring to boil on medium-high heat. Reduce heat to low; simmer 10 minutes. Sprinkle 2 Tablespoons cheese onto bottom of each serving bowl; top with chili. Sprinkle each with additional 2 Tablespoons cheese.

Hindsight 20/20

I once had a friend who was in desperate need of a job. She had been laid off and she was running out of money fast. They were hiring for one position where I worked so I encouraged her to apply. We both thought it would be fun to work together. She got a first interview and then a second interview, and I was sure she would soon be hired. I remember the day she called me in tears because she didn't get the job. She was devastated. The company had decided to go with a male candidate instead. I couldn't believe it; she was certainly qualified with more than ten years of experience. I decided I should meet the guy who "stole" this job from my friend so I made a point to seek him out and introduce myself. I was sure he would turn out to be some cocky college kid with a serious attitude problem. How wrong I was......

Have you heard the story of the man who spent every penny he had to buy a horse, only to have the horse run away? All the neighbors said"Oh, that's bad." But the man said, "How do you know it's bad, maybe it's good." Then the horse returned bringing with him a second horse doubling the man's fortune. All the neighbors congratulated the man saying, "Oh that's good!" But the man said, "How do you know that's good, maybe that's bad." While riding one day the man's son fell from the horse severely breaking his leg and the neighbors said "Oh, that's bad." But the man said "How do you know that's bad, maybe that's good." A year later the war began and the army drafted all the able bodied men to be soldiers. The man's son was left home because of his disabled leg. This story could go on forever but I am sure you get the point. To know if a situation is good or bad you really need the benefit of time. My grandma called it "Hindsight 20/20." I call it foresight.

Can you imagine the choices we would make if only we had foresight as a superpower? Forget the flying cape, foresight would be great! We'd know which investments to make; seriously did you think a blanket with arms called a "Snuggie" would be a top seller? (In my day a snuggie was something you wanted to avoid at all costs!) We'd know which houses to buy, which jobs to take and so on – we would never make a mistake. I think foresight should be right up there with the invisibility cloak. (Also, a favorite of mine.) By now you're probably wondering whatever happened to my friend? Heartbroken and unemployed she turned to shopping for comfort, ended up in serious credit card debt, borrowed a *boat load* of money from me and never paid it back. (I seriously misjudged her character.) And what about the guy who "stole" her job? As it turned out he was handsome, smart and funny, so I married him. Who could have seen that coming? Happy Anniversary Mike!

"Meeting you was fate. Becoming your friend was my choice. But baby, falling in love with you was beyond my control." Unknown

Here are some delicious recipes made with a simple brownie mix. Only time will tell if these will become family favorites!

Caramelized Pecan Brownies

1 package chewy brownie mix (recommended: Duncan Hines)
4 Tablespoons butter
1 cup chopped pecans
1 cup firmly packed light brown sugar

Preheat oven to 350 degrees. Prepare the brownie mix according to the package directions. Pour batter into a greased 9 by 13 pan. Melt the butter in a small saucepan. Add the pecans and sugar and cook, over medium heat, stirring frequently, until the sugar dissolves. Drizzle the caramel mixture over brownie batter and bake until a toothpick can be inserted and withdrawn cleanly, 25 to 30 minutes.

Peanut Butter Cup Brownie Cupcakes

1 (15 ounce) package Brownie mix (any variety)
⅓ cup very hot water
¼ cup oil
1 egg
12 miniature peanut butter cups, unwrapped

Preheat oven to 350 degrees. Line a muffin pan with 12 cupcake papers. Combine brownie mix, water, oil, and egg. Beat 50 strokes. Fill muffin cups two thirds full. Press an unwrapped mini peanut butter cup into the batter until top edge of candy is even with batter. Bake for 20 to 30 minutes until brownie is set. Cool. My friend Betsy made this recipe for our book club meeting and it was beyond delicious! No one would ever know it's made with a package brownie mix, unless of course they had hindsight!

Cherry Fudge Cheesecake Dessert

1 box (1 lb 2.4 oz) Betty Crocker® Original Supreme Premium brownie mix (With the chocolate syrup pouch)
3 Tablespoons butter, melted
2 packages (8 ounces each) cream cheese, softened
1 ½ cups whipping (heavy) cream
1 can (21 ounces) cherry pie filling (you can also use raspberry or strawberry pie filling – yum!)

Heat oven to 350 degrees. Stir together one and a half cups of the dry, unprepared brownie mix, and the melted butter. Press in bottom of an ungreased spring form pan, or a 9 by 9 square pan.

Beat cream cheese in large bowl with electric mixer on medium speed about 2 minutes, scraping bowl frequently, until smooth. Add remaining dry brownie mix, the whipping cream and chocolate syrup. Beat on medium speed, scraping bowl frequently, until smooth. Pour over crust in pan.

Bake 45 to 50 minutes for spring form pan, 35 to 40 minutes for nine inch square pan, or until set; cool 20 minutes. Run metal spatula along side of cheesecake to loosen before and after refrigerating. Spread pie filling over cheesecake. Cover and refrigerate until chilled, about 2 hours. Cover and refrigerate any remaining cheesecake.

Sick and Tired of Being
Sick and Tired

Usually I try to be a glass half full kind of gal; but seriously having a cold for ten plus days can really dampen a person's spirits. And how is it Tylenol Cold tablets know EXACTLY when four hours have passed? I swear I could set my clock by my cold medicine wearing off. (2:00 am and 6:00 am to be specific). My oldest son has also had a rough winter with colds, flu's and a serious case of Epstein Barr Syndrome. (EBS is a really long name for mono.) The upside to this was that the hospital lab tech, after drawing his blood on three separate occasions, adopted our naughty little Chihuahua and they now live happily together in Orono. (The other day I actually opened all the doors and windows for a full 25 minutes just to air out the house. It didn't matter that I had to crank up the fireplace, as it was only 16 degrees, it sure felt a lot fresher.) We are all just sick and tired of being sick and tired!

I remember my parent's home remedies for colds and fevers. They thought it was best to sweat it out so Dad would pile a bunch of quilts on top of us while mom whipped up a cup of her "cold killer." Hot lemonade with a touch of brandy. (Eww!) God forbid if you were caught sticking a toe out from under the blankets. Another remedy was to grease us down with Watkins Menthol Camphor Ointment rub she bought from Mrs. Lewis across the road. Mom would spread it on our back, throat, chest and a huge gob right under your nose where you had to smell it. I have read now where rubbing Vicks on the bottom of your feet and putting socks on will work to clear up a sore throat. Who knew?

I found some great cold remedies in an old book last week. I thought I would share them with you in case you are brave at heart. Minced fresh garlic spread on toast, Cayenne pepper tea, hot red wine with a dash of black pepper, or drink a mixture of garlic oil and onion juice and warm fried onions plastered on your chest. My personal favorite was to place your hat on the table and drink from a large bottle of whisky until you see <u>two hats</u> then get into bed and stay there! Some of these cures sound worse than the disease! A sure fire way to feel better is to have a sense of humor. Did you hear about the man who went to see his doctor because he was suffering from a miserable cold? His doctor prescribed some pills, but they didn't help. On his next visit the doctor gave him a shot, but that didn't do any good. On his third visit the doctor told the man to go home and take a hot bath. As soon as he was finished bathing he was to throw open all the windows and stands in the draft. "But doc," protested the patient, "if I do that, I'll get pneumonia." "I know," said his physician. "I can cure pneumonia." Ha! Let's hope we all feel better soon!

Here are some recipes that are probably not your Grandma's Chicken Soup. All are delicious, easy to make and good for whatever ails you.

Coconut Lime Chicken Soup

2 pounds deli roasted chicken
1 (15 ounce) can unsweetened coconut milk
2 cups water
¼ cup lime juice (2 medium limes)
3 medium carrots, thinly sliced
1 Tablespoon soy sauce
2 teaspoon Thai seasoning blend
¼ teaspoon salt
Fresh cilantro, optional
Lime wedges optional

Remove and discard skin and bones from chicken. Shred chicken. In large saucepan combine shredded chicken with coconut milk, water, lime juice, sliced carrots, soy sauce, 2 teaspoons Thai seasoning and salt. Bring to boil; reduce heat and simmer, covered, 8 minutes or until carrots are crisp-tender. To serve, sprinkle bowls of soup with additional Thai seasoning and cilantro. Pass lime wedges.

Sweet and Sour Chicken Soup

6 cups Chicken Stock
2 Tablespoons rice vinegar
2 Tablespoons low sodium soy sauce
1 teaspoon minced peeled fresh ginger
1 teaspoon bottled minced garlic
½ teaspoon salt
⅛ teaspoon pepper
1 (3.5 ounce) package shiitake mushrooms, stems removed and thinly sliced
2 cups shredded cooked chicken
2 cups thinly sliced spinach leaves
1 ½ ounces wheat noodles or angel hair pasta, uncooked

Combine first 8 ingredients in a large Dutch oven; bring to a boil. Cover, reduce heat, and simmer 30 minutes. Stir in chicken, spinach, and noodles; cook 5 minutes.

Latin Chicken Soup

1 Tablespoon vegetable oil
2 cloves garlic, chopped
2 medium carrots, chopped
2 medium stalks celery, chopped
1 medium onion, chopped
½ jalapeño Chile with seeds, thinly sliced

1 teaspoon ground cumin
1 carton (32 ounces) chicken broth (4 cups)
1 ½ cups water
1 cup corn kernels
2 Tablespoons fresh lime juice
2 cups shredded skinless rotisserie chicken meat
½ cups loosely packed fresh cilantro leaves, coarsely chopped
2 plum tomatoes, chopped
1 ripe medium avocado, cut into half-inch pieces
Lime wedges
Tortilla chips

In 5 to 6 quart saucepot, heat oil over low heat until hot. Add garlic, carrots, celery, onion and jalapeno, and cook covered, 8 to 10 minutes or until vegetables are tender, stir frequently. Add cumin and cook 30 seconds, stirring. Add broth and water to vegetable mixture; cover saucepot and bring back to a boil. Stir corn kernels, lime juice, chicken pieces, and chopped cilantro into broth mixture in saucepot; heat to boiling over high heat. Remove saucepot from heat; stir in chopped tomatoes. Ladle soup into 4 warm large soup bowls; sprinkle with avocado pieces. Serve with lime wedges to squeeze over soup. Accompany with tortilla chips to crush into soup if you like.

The Beauty Within

One of my favorite short stories comes from a man named Moses.
Moses was not a handsome man. He was short and he also had
a hunched back. When he met a beautiful young lady named
Frumtje, Moses fell madly in love, but Frumtje was repulsed by
his appearance and his hunched back. Finally getting the courage
to talk to her, Moses asked, "Do you believe that all marriages are
made in heaven?" When she said yes, Moses said, "In heaven at the
birth of each boy, the Lord announces which girl he will marry.
When I was born, my future bride was pointed out to me. Then
the Lord said, 'But your wife will be humpbacked.' Right then
and there I called out, 'Oh Lord, a humpbacked woman would be
a tragedy. _Please, Lord, let her be **beautiful and give me the hump**._"
Frumtje became his devoted wife. Can you imagine a gesture
more beautiful than this? Not only was Moses a hunchback, he
was a smooth talker. No wonder Frumtje fell in love with him.
He had an inner beauty.

I was recently reminded of this story as I read "The Little
Locksmith." This is an autobiography about young girl fighting
Pott's disease where without treatment she would become a
hunchback. So her family kept her bedridden from the age of
five to the age of fifteen to try to prevent the inevitable. (Ten
years in bed. Flat on her back.) When I originally suggested this
novel for my book club I thought it would be a tragic account of
her bedridden life and how much she suffered. I was so wrong.
Katharine Butler Hathaway had a writing style to be admired.
You want to read her words slowly, absorbing every phrase and
quote. My very favorite is her description of a good friend being
a "gardener of human beings". She felt that the most difficult
"human" plants are in the wrong places suffering drought, heat,

or dampness. If only a noticing, intuitive hand of a friend could move among them, they each might flourish as they were meant to. Her friend never saw her delicate health or her disfigurement; she only spoke of her beauty and of her talents. Wouldn't this be the greatest of compliments, to be called a gardener of human beings and to help people discover their own inner beauty? For Katharine there was nothing better than the encouragement of a good friend.

How often we see the darkness of those around us. If only we could place our focus on the positive? And if only we could build up, encourage one another, and support each other's talents; both those apparent and those they keep well hidden. Sometimes we have to look beyond the "hunchback" to see the beauty within.

*"Inner beauty is a kind of radiance. You can see the people who possess a true **inner beauty**, their eyes are a little brighter, their skin a little more dewy. They vibrate at a different frequency." ~ Cameron Diaz*

Wonderful cakes with beautiful fillings "within".

Chocolate Raspberry Bundt Cake

Batter:
1 cup melted butter
2 eggs
2 cups sugar
1 cup milk
1 cup water
1 teaspoon vanilla
3 cups flour
¾ cup cocoa
2 teaspoons baking powder
¼ teaspoon salt

Filling:

12 ounces cream cheese, softened

⅓ cup sugar

1 cup chocolate chips

1 teaspoon vanilla

1 ½ cups fresh raspberries

Preheat oven to 375 degrees. Grease a Bundt or tube pan. Make filling by creaming together, cream cheese with sugar and vanilla. Mix in chocolate chips and set aside. For cake, sift together the flour, cocoa, baking powder and salt. Beat eggs and gradually add the sugar and beat until the mixture is thick and pale yellow. Beat in melted butter, then milk, water and vanilla. Gradually add in the flour mixture and mix well. Spread half the batter into the prepared pan. Drop spoonfuls of the cream cheese filling evenly over the batter. Sprinkle raspberries over the top. Cover with remaining batter. Bake 60 to 75 minutes

Chocolate Macaroon Bundt Cake

2 cups sifted all-purpose flour

2 cups white sugar, divided

½ cup unsweetened cocoa powder

1 teaspoon salt

1 teaspoon baking soda

2 teaspoons vanilla extract

¼ cup water

½ cup shortening

½ cup sour cream

4 eggs, divided

1 cup flaked coconut

1 Tablespoon all-purpose flour

1 teaspoon vanilla extract

Glaze:

3 Tablespoons cocoa powdered

2 Tablespoons melted butter

1 cup powdered sugar

2 Tablespoons hot water

Preheat oven to 350 degrees. Grease and flour a 10 inch Bundt pan.

Filling: Beat 1 egg white in a small bowl until peaks form. Gradually beat in ¼ cup sugar. Beat until stiff peaks form. Fold in coconut, 1 Tablespoon flour and 1 teaspoon vanilla. Set aside.

Batter: In a large bowl, mix together flour, 1 ¾ cups sugar, cocoa, salt and soda. Add vanilla, water, shortening, sour cream 4 egg yolks and 3 egg whites. Blend at low speed until moistened, and then beat at medium speed for 3 minutes. Chocolate Glaze: Mix cocoa, butter, powdered sugar and hot water.

Pour cake batter into Bundt pan. Drop the filling by teaspoons around the top of the batter, avoiding the edges. Bake 55 to 60 minutes, or until a toothpick inserted into the center of the cake comes out clean. Let it cool in the pan for 10 minutes, and then turn out onto a wire rack to continue cooling. Top with Chocolate Glaze:

Apple Bundt Cake

2 cups apples - peeled, cored and diced

1 Tablespoon white sugar

1 teaspoon ground cinnamon

3 cups all-purpose flour

3 teaspoons baking powder

½ teaspoon salt

2 cups sugar

1 cup vegetable oil

¼ cup orange juice

2 ½ teaspoons vanilla extract

4 eggs

1 cup chopped walnuts

¼ cup powdered sugar for dusting

Preheat oven to 350 degrees. Grease and flour a 10 inch Bundt or tube pan. In a medium bowl, combine the diced apples, 1 Tablespoon white sugar and 1 teaspoon cinnamon; set aside. Sift together the flour, baking powder and salt; set aside. In a large bowl, combine 2 cups sugar, oil, orange juice, vanilla and eggs. Beat at high speed until smooth. Stir in flour mixture. Fold in chopped walnuts. Pour one third of the batter into prepared pan. Sprinkle with one half of the apple mixture. Alternate layers of batter and filling, ending with batter. Bake for 55 to 60 minutes, or until the top springs back when lightly touched. Let cool in pan for 10 minutes, then turn out onto a wire rack and cool completely. Sprinkle with powdered sugar.

On Eagles Wings

Most people spend a lot of time (and money) trying to attract birds to their yard or interact with them in nature. I love to feed the birds and I get very excited when a bluebird or cardinal couple decides to nest in our back yard. Seriously, I bet I put out about 50 gallons of hummingbird juice every summer. Some of it is drunk by a raccoon with a taste for red hooch but most of it goes to feed these little wonders of nature. (We have three hummingbird feeders and if you get too close they will buzz you like giant bees.) But never in my wildest dreams did I think a bald eagle couple would take up nesting in my back yard. Well they didn't. They landed at the home of Mary Ellen and Willard Holthaus in Decorah, Iowa. Yes, my mother and father-in-law. It all started about four years ago during a terrible wind storm. A pair of bald eagles lost their nesting tree across the road from the Holt-house. My brother-in-law went over to check out the broken nest on the ground and it was HUGE. (Can you believe a bald eagle nest weighs more than a ton?) Within a couple of days the eagles found a new branch high in a Cottonwood tree that seemed sturdy enough and that branch just happened to be in my in-laws yard! The eagles spent a couple of weeks building their new home and then came the first egg. That was in 2008.

The nest became a popular local attraction in Decorah and then in 2009 Bob Anderson from the Raptor Resource Project asked my in-laws if he could put an eagle camera in the nest and use their garage to house his equipment. They agreed. The camera provides a live feed of a wild mating pair of bald eagles. The male, the slightly smaller eagle, and the female take turns sitting on the eggs and caring for their young hatchlings. Who would have guessed that today more than 136,000 viewers would be watching three baby hatchlings and their parents at any given time? (They panned the yard the other day and Mary Ellen had her laundry on the clothes line. I am sure she didn't appreciate having her laundry viewed by people in 130 countries <u>around the world</u>! Ha!) To me the camera makes the nest seem kind of small but it is more than six feet long and six feet deep. When they put the cameras up in the tree the cameraman lay down in the nest and stretched out full length!

Many schools are using the eagle camera as a teaching tool, and Bob Anderson said he has had a lot of people tell him they like to keep the live camera feed going for hours. Some of these people have told him they're sick and in pain but that they find watching the eagles' soo relaxing they forget about their illness. Isn't that amazing? If you ask my mother in law about the eagles she can only find one downside, when the baby eagles start to fly they like to land on the TV antenna and that doesn't hold them up very well. To date the Decorah eagle camera has had more than 7 million viewers! Now here's my plan…if each viewer would just send me $1.00 (plus shipping and handling) I would send them a guaranteed authentic <u>photo copy</u> of real eagle tracks!

 Just kidding, you can have these for free.

<u>Seven Layer Eagle Bars</u>

½ cup butter, melted
1 ½ cups graham cracker crumbs
1 (14 ounce) can EAGLE Sweetened Condensed Milk
1 cup semisweet chocolate morsels
1 cup butterscotch chips
1 cup flaked coconut
1 cup chopped nuts

243

Heat oven to 350 degrees (325 degrees for glass dish). Coat 9 by 13 pan with nonstick cooking spray. Combine graham cracker crumbs and butter. Press into bottom of prepared pan. Pour sweetened condensed milk evenly over crumb mixture. Layer evenly with chocolate chips, coconut and nuts. Press down firmly with a fork. Bake 25 minutes or until lightly browned. Cool. Cut into bars or diamonds. Store covered at room temperature.

Eagle Pumpkin Bars

1 ½ cups flour
1 cup finely chopped nuts
½ cup sugar
½ cup firmly packed brown sugar
2 teaspoons ground cinnamon, divided
¾ cup butter, softened
1 (15 ounce) can pumpkin
1 (14 ounce) can EAGLE Sweetened Condensed Milk
2 eggs, beaten
½ teaspoon ground allspice
¼ teaspoon salt
1 Tablespoon flour

Preheat oven to 375 degrees. In medium bowl, combine flour, nuts, sugars and 1 teaspoon cinnamon. Add butter, mix until crumbly. Reserve 1 ¼ cups of the mixture. Pat remaining mixture on bottom of an ungreased 9 by 13 pan. Meanwhile, in large mixing bowl, combine pumpkin, sweetened condensed milk, eggs, remaining 1 teaspoon cinnamon, allspice and salt; mix well. Pour evenly over crust. Mix reserved crumbs with 1 Tablespoon flour. Sprinkle over pumpkin mixture.
Bake 30 to 35 minutes or until set. Cool 10 minutes. Serve warm. Store leftovers in refrigerator.

Eagle Key Lime Pie

4 large eggs, separated
1 (14 ounce) can EAFLE Sweetened Condensed Milk
½ cup fresh lime juice
¾ cup heavy cream
1 teaspoon grated lime peel
2 or 3 drops green food coloring
1 (nine-inch) unbaked pie crust
½ teaspoon cream of tartar
½ cup sugar

Heat oven to 350 degrees. Beat egg yolks in medium bowl on low speed of electric mixer. Gradually beat in sweetened condensed milk and lime juice until smooth. Blend in cream, lime peel and food coloring, if desired. Pour into unbaked pie crust. Bake 25 minutes. Remove from oven. Beat egg whites and cream of tartar in medium bowl on high speed until soft peaks form. Gradually beat in sugar on medium speed. Beat 4 minutes or until sugar is dissolved and stiff glossy peaks form. Spread over hot pie, carefully sealing to edge of crust to prevent meringue from shrinking. Bake an additional 15 minutes or until meringue is lightly browned. Cool 1 hour on wire rack. Chill at least 3 hours before serving.

What's Up Doc?

Beginning with my days of watching early morning cartoons until today I have loved carrots. My brother and I would munch along with Bugs Bunny on Saturday morning and I am sure my mom heard "What's up Doc" more times than she could shake a stick at. What is it about a carrot that makes it so inviting? For one, it's orange. Not boring white like the potato or faded green like the inside of those awful zucchinis. (Yuck!) Carrots are bright and sweet and crunchy and delicious. And my friend they are really fun to grow; the seeds come up fast and there is no waiting for them to ripen. If you have never pulled a carrot straight from the garden, wiped off the dirt and eaten it standing in the sun, you have not truly lived. Carrot seeds are really small though, and I thought they were hard to plant until I found this great invention, seed tape. What you spend on the tape saves you money on all the wasted seeds you drop in the dirt trying to sort them out. Less thinning too. My kids liked to pull the carrots fresh from the garden and feed them to the horses. I would always remind them to hold their hands really flat so the horse didn't think their little fingers were baby carrots! This usually caused some eye rolling and giggles but seriously who knows what a horse is thinking?

I don't know why years ago people thought they had to mix shredded carrots with lime Jello to get us to enjoy this vegetable. Come on, green and orange don't even go together in an outfit unless your want to look like a pumpkin. And why would imitation lime flavored Jello be a compliment to the delicious taste of a carrot? Forgive me if this is a favorite salad of yours but what can I say...I just don't find it appealing or tasty. When I plant carrots now I like to try a couple of different kinds. Some are super sweet and I tried one last year that was a little spicy.

This year I am going to try to grow a new short, round carrot that resembles the shape of a radish. These are supposedly good for people that have harder soil and carrots can't grow long and thin in the dirt. I even found seed for purple and white carrots on the Internet that look fun. I know Bugs would shudder and probably say "What the <u>heck</u> is up Doc?"? if I were to hand him a purple carrot but it might look better in lime Jello. Then again, maybe not.

There are two rumors about carrots I feel I need to dispel right now. Baby carrots you buy in the store are truly not young, small, tender carrots. These "mini" carrots are cut and shaped into "baby" carrots from long fully grown carrots. That's why they don't always taste sweet and fresh. Rumor two, Mel Blanc, the voice of Bugs Bunny was <u>not</u> allergic to carrots. He didn't swallow them during recording sessions because chewing and eating the carrot took too much time. And for all those children out there who doubt the wisdom of their mothers: a lady in Annandale told me her sister, who happens to live in Grand Marais, was feeding her horse when it bit off her finger and swallowed it! I just knew fingers look like carrots! As my mom would say "You should listen to me, I'm not as dumb as I look."

"Don't take life too seriously. You'll never get out alive." - Bugs Bunny

<u>Grandma Isabelle Allard's Carrot Cake</u>

Batter:
4 eggs
1 ¼ cups vegetable oil
2 cups sugar
2 teaspoons vanilla
2 cups flour
2 teaspoons baking soda
2 teaspoons baking powder
½ teaspoon salt

2 teaspoons ground cinnamon
3 cups grated carrots
1 cup chopped pecans
1 cup raisins

Frosting:
½ cup butter, softened (Do not use margarine)
8 ounces cream cheese, softened
4 cups powdered sugar
1 teaspoon vanilla extract
1 cup chopped pecans (OPTIONAL)

Preheat oven to 350 degrees. Grease and flour a 9 by 13 pan. In a large bowl, beat together eggs, oil, sugar and 2 teaspoons vanilla. Mix in flour, baking soda, baking powder, salt and cinnamon. Stir in carrots. Fold in pecans. Pour into prepared pan. Bake for 40 to 50 minutes, or until a toothpick inserted into the center of the cake comes out clean. Let cool in pan for 10 minutes, then turn out onto a wire rack and cool completely.

Frosting: In a medium bowl, combine butter, cream cheese, powdered sugar and 1 teaspoon vanilla. Beat until the mixture is smooth and creamy. Stir in chopped pecans. Frost the cooled cake.

Easy Maple Glazed Carrots

8 Medium sized carrots or two cups baby carrots
½ cup orange juice
3 Tablespoons maple syrup
1 pinch of nutmeg
3 Tablespoons butter

Peel carrots; cut into sticks. Pour the orange juice into a 4 cup microwave safe dish. Heat 1 minute on high. Add the carrots. Stir to coat the carrots with the orange juice. Cover and microwave

8 to 9 minutes on high. Stir again, and then add the remaining ingredients. Microwave, uncovered 2 minutes on high. Stir, and then check for doneness. If necessary, cook another 1 minute on High.

The BEST Carrot Soup

2 pounds peeled or scrubbed, chopped carrots
4 cups stock, vegetable or chicken
1 teaspoon salt
1 medium potato, peeled and chopped
3 to 4 Tablespoons butter
1 cup chopped onion, divided
1 to 2 small cloves crushed garlic
⅓ cup chopped cashews
½ pint heavy cream OR ¾ cup sour cream
1 teaspoon each of thyme, marjoram and basil

Place carrots and half of the onion, liquid stock and salt and potato into a medium sized pot and bring to a boil. Cover and simmer for 12 to 15 minutes. Let it cool to room temp.

In a frying pan sauté the rest of the onion, garlic and nuts in the butter until the onions are clear. You can sprinkle in a little salt to help draw the moisture out of the onions. Towards the end of cooking, stir in the seasonings. Set aside until serving time.

Puree the carrots and potato together in a blender until smooth. Return to pan and gently reheat, then add heavy cream OR sour cream and stir. Do not boil. Serve with onion nut mixture on top.

Café's before There Were Lattes

I grew up just a mile from the Cross River Café in Schroeder. (Don't look for it now, it burned down several years ago….) I wish it was still there because I think every small town grows closer together if they have a cafe. Where else do you meet and greet over a cup of coffee? Café's have a way of making you feel like Norm in Cheers. (Everybody knows your name.) Walking in can feel like coming home but even better because you know someone else will be doing the dishes. (Although my Dad's favorite threat was to send us in back to wash dishes to work off our bill.) At the Cross River Café there was a counter with stools that twirled around (until your mom said stop), a front hall with huge windows, and a back room for "fine" dining. In the 50's and 60's it was called "Smith's Café" and my mom worked there while she was in high school. When I worked at Lambs grocery store across the river I would take my lunch breaks at the café. Every day I ordered a tuna sandwich on toast with cheese. (Still my favorite lunch to this day.)

When I graduated from high school, I moved to the campground in Grand Marais and worked at the Blue Water Café. (This was my second experience working at a restaurant because I had started out working at Satellites Country Inn the year before. Satellites didn't have a counter with stools but it did have a customer table where you could sit if you came in alone and wanted to visit. The truck drivers liked to sit there. They taught me to eat my French fries dipped in brown gravy!) At the Blue Water Café I soon learned the regular customer's favorites and could put in their order with only a nod. One lady had a grilled cheese sandwich dipped in yellow mustard every time she came in. (This I never developed a taste for even though I tried it once.) The cook at Blue Water would also make the best desserts; lemon bars to die for and pecan pie! I had never before tried pecan pie but once I did I was hooked. After a shift, there was nothing better than sitting down to a piece of pie and a cup of hot coffee.

Where I live now in Annandale I guess you could say I am a regular breakfast customer at Homestyle Café. I like to meet my friends there on Tuesday mornings. The waitress, Kelly, knows my order by heart…two poached eggs with English muffin toast and hot water – I bring my own tea bags in my purse. Usually at least one other customer greets me by name and says hello. It reminds me of my youth and the friendliness you only get in a small town. I also enjoy a good cup of tea at In Hot Water about one day a week. I hope we have places around Annandale for years to come. Besides I am betting if I tried spinning on one of the counter stools I might get away with it longer now than I did with my mom.

"Strangely enough, the first character in Fried Green Tomatoes was the cafe, and the town. I think a place can be as much a character in a novel as the people." ~ Fannie Flagg

Rhubarb Cherry Dessert – from Astrid Gottschalk

Filling:
4 cups chopped fresh rhubarb
½ cup sugar
3 Tablespoons flour

2 Tablespoons cornstarch
1 cup sugar
1 cup cold water

1 (21 ounce) can cherry pie filling
1 teaspoon almond extract

Crust:
¾ cup butter
1 ½ cups flour
1 ½ cups oatmeal
¼ cup packed brown sugar
¼ teaspoon salt

Combine the rhubarb with ½ cup sugar and the flour. Let sit overnight. Boil 1 cup sugar, water and cornstarch until thick then add to rhubarb mixture. Add the almond flavoring to the cherry pie filling, keep separate. Make the crust mixture.

For crust combine ingredients and pat half the mixture into a 9 by 13 pan. Pour the rhubarb mixture over the crust; spoon the cherry mixture over all and sprinkle top with rest of crust mixture. Bake at 350 degrees for 45 minutes.

Rhubarb-Buttermilk Muffins

Batter:
1 ½ cups brown sugar
¼ cup oil
1 egg
2 teaspoon vanilla
1 cup buttermilk
1 ½ cups finely diced rhubarb
½ cups pecan pieces (optional)
2 ½ cups flour
1 teaspoon baking powder
1 teaspoon baking soda
½ teaspoon salt

Topping:
⅓ cup sugar

1 ½ teaspoon cinnamon
1 Tablespoon melted butter

Preheat oven to 400 degrees. Grease 24 medium sized muffin cups. Combine in large bowl: brown sugar, oil, egg, and vanilla. Beat until well mixed. Stir in buttermilk, rhubarb, and pecans. In another bowl, sift together flour, baking powder, baking soda, and salt. Add this mixture all at once to rhubarb mixture and stir until all ingredients are moistened. Do not over mix. Fill prepared muffin pan ¾ full with batter. Combine topping ingredients and sprinkle on top of batter in each muffin cup. Bake in preheated oven on center shelf 15 to 20 minutes.

Rhubarb and Raspberry Tart

2 cups rhubarb
1 cup raspberries
¾ cup sugar
3 eggs
1 egg yolk
½ cup whipping cream
⅓ teaspoon vanilla
1 pre made pie crust for ten-inch shell

Raspberries and rhubarb in one tart means that one of the fruits must be frozen, otherwise it cooks to mush. Happily, this dish works well with either fresh or frozen berries or rhubarb. The reds and pinks are beautiful together and the flavors blend wonderfully. Roll out pie dough into ten-inch pie pan. Cut rhubarb into quarter inch pieces, distribute evenly in tart shell, and then sprinkle with raspberries. Combine sugar, eggs and egg yolk in a mixing bowl; whisk ingredients together. Add cream and vanilla and mix. Pour egg mixture over fruit and bake in preheated oven at 400 degrees for 20 to 25 minutes, or until tart batter is quite firm.

For the Love of a Pet

My daughter Zoë leaves for college in less than a month yet she continues to grow her collection of pets. She insists that these are her pets, not mine; but you and I both know who will be feeding them, cleaning up after them and overall caring for them after she's left....yup me. Do I have "easy mark" tattooed on my forehead? The latest was introduced to me via a text pictures on my cell phone. Zoë holding a white rat. I texted back "No Way." Then a close up photo of just his whiskered little face. "Not in my house." I replied. The final photo was of Zoë with a rat sitting on her shoulder, in the car! Seriously, was my phone not working? Were my messages lost in cyberspace? She named him Atticus. (Yes after Gregory Peck in To Kill a Mockingbird though Atticus the rat does not look like a lawyer or anything like Gregory Peck.) Just to set the record straight he is not living here once she goes to college. He will have to pack his little rat bags and rent somewhere, maybe closer to town. Regal name or not, I will not be swayed. I am not a rat keeper. Did I mention she has two cats, a rabbit and a turtle that she is leaving in my care? (See I am not totally heartless.)

I think pets are wonderful teaching tools for kids and great companions. We have had cats, kittens, fish, turtles, hamsters, rabbits, bunnies, birds, dogs, puppies, horses, chickens, ducks, alpacas and a llama. I have paid my pet dues. Now I would like to downsize. Let's face it, I am tired and a rat is not up there on my list of favorite pets. I don't even think they would be in the top ten. I least I can thank my lucky stars it is not a snake. I do need to warn you the day a snake moves in here, I move out. It's not even a concept I can consider. Call it irrational, I fear snakes. Though I have never had a bad experience with a snake but I think it was seeing my mother run screaming from a snake when I was young that imprinted it on my brain. One should never touch a snake, let alone share a house with one.

Ok those of you who knew me in my younger days might remember I had pet mice so you might think it hypocritical of me to send this little rat packing... (a pack rat sent packing, ha-ha!...) but if you remember my two tiny mice (Pickin' and Grinnin' after Hee Haw characters) grew into about 25 mice in a very short period of time. Soon I had a cage full of mice and it quickly turned into a big to-do at my house when they all escaped. (We captured most of them but my mother swore she would see a spotted mouse out in the yard for years to come.) So in my defense, pets are great "teaching tools" and therefore I am not going to risk an invasion of rodents of any kind in my home. God love my mother for letting me have all my pets but I think she really did have "easy mark" tattooed on <u>her</u> forehead.

> *"You can't be friends with a squirrel! A squirrel is just a rat with a cuter outfit!"* ~Sarah Jessica Parker

Simple Chick Pea Recipes

Keep a few cans of chick peas (Garbanzo Beans) on hand and you will always be ready to serve up one of these delicious recipes in a snap.

<u>Roasted Chick Peas</u>

2 Tablespoons olive oil
1 Tablespoon ground cumin
1 teaspoon garlic powder
½ teaspoon chili powder
1 pinch sea salt
1 pinch ground black pepper

1 dash crushed red pepper
1 (15 ounce) can chickpeas, rinsed and drained

Preheat oven to 350 degrees. Whisk the oil, cumin, garlic powder, chili powder, sea salt, black pepper, and red pepper together in a small bowl; add the chickpeas and toss to coat. Spread into a single layer on a baking sheet. Roast in the preheated oven, stirring occasionally, until nicely browned and slightly crispy, about 45 minutes.

Chick Pea Coconut Salad

1 (15 ounce) can garbanzo beans (chickpeas), rinsed and drained
⅓ cup freshly grated coconut
⅓ cup chopped fresh cilantro
2 teaspoons lemon juice
½ teaspoon salt

Combine garbanzo beans, coconut, and cilantro in a large bowl. Stir in lemon juice, and season with salt. Refrigerate for 2 hours before serving for best flavor.

Chick Pea and Black Bean Hummus

1 cup canned black beans, drained
1 cup canned garbanzo beans (chickpeas), drained
1 Tablespoon olive oil
2 Tablespoons fresh lemon juice
2 Tablespoons plain nonfat yogurt
2 Tablespoons water
1 clove garlic, roughly chopped
1 ½ teaspoons curry powder
Salt and pepper to taste

Place black beans, garbanzo beans, olive oil, lemon juice, yogurt, water, and garlic into the bowl of a blender. Season with curry powder, salt, and pepper. Cover and puree until smooth. Refrigerate until ready to serve.

No, Your Daddy is Not the Schwann's Man

I was thinking today that if someone asked me to pick only one dessert that I could have the rest of my life, what would it be? Hands down I would say ice cream then I would have unlimited delicious choices of flavors and novelties! Just today I had a wonderful root beer float in downtown Annandale. It was my duty as this was a school fundraiser for the cheerleaders. (True confession: I actually had two root beer floats because I brought one home for my son but he was asleep and I didn't want it to go to waste.) I think I have passed my love of ice cream on to my children as well. When the Schwann's truck pulls up they can order by novelty numbers....013 (orange push-ups) and 044 (chocolate chip ice cream sandwiches) are often called out while he is punching in our order. (Makes a mother proud doesn't it?) If we happen to miss our Schwann's day there is often weeping and it's not just the kids.

This food fetish I blame on my parents who often had ice cream as a bedtime snack. New York Vanilla with Nestles Quik on top. When you let it get all melty and stir it up it's like a malt in a bowl. I was sharing this story with my son as we were parked at the Peppermint Twist in Delano this week. Whenever we go to Delano I feel it is my personal responsibility to support the Peppermint Twist. If I don't, I am afraid it will close and I don't know of any other place where you can sit in your car, order over a speakerphone and have a waitress deliver it to the car window. (Just like Happy Days!) It looks kind of goofy with pink painted bears dancing on the lawn but hands down, they serve the best malts in the area. When I was young there was an A&W Root

Beer restaurant in Grand Marais that also served you at your car window. It was a really big deal to get root beer in a teeny tiny frosted mug. Something about a frosty mug adds to the root beer sensation. (Word of advice – do not drink root beer through a tiny straw – it will come out your nose. I speak from experience….)

Some of my greatest memories are tied to ice cream. Once on a trip to Maine I picked fresh raspberries then ate them with lemon custard ice cream. It tastes so good I almost cried. Another is eating Dove bars and orange popsicles sitting by a fan at my little house in South Minneapolis…no air conditioning so I had an excuse to eat as many as I wanted, guilt free! How about Bananas Foster? (Flaming bananas over vanilla ice cream. Yum!) I joked on Facebook the other day that I should have married a Schwann's Man. One of my high school friends reminded me that she was married to a Schwann's man once…they had THE MOST beautiful ice cream babies but the relationship cooled off quickly! Ha! Seize the moment, eat ice cream.

> *"Remember all those women on the Titanic who*
> *waved off the dessert cart." ~Erma Bombeck*

Apple Ice Cream Pie

1 large store bought graham cracker crust
2 Tablespoons unsalted butter
3 Golden Delicious apples, peeled, cored, and cut into one-inch chunks
¼ cup powdered sugar, sifted
1 ½ Tablespoons fresh lemon juice
1 (12 ounce) jar caramel topping
1 quart vanilla ice cream
½ cup chopped walnuts or pecans, toasted (optional)

Read the package directions on the graham cracker crust and prebake if necessary. You can, of course, use your favorite homemade crust recipe, pressed into a nine-inch pie pan and prebake. In either case, let the crust cool on a cooling rack while you prepare the apples. Melt the butter in a large nonreactive skillet or sauté pan. Add the apples and cook, stirring, over medium heat until they're just about tender, 5 to 6 minutes. Stir in the powdered sugar and lemon juice, cook for another minute or so, and remove from the heat. Let cool. When the apples are almost cool, scrape them and their juice into the pie shell, spreading them evenly in the crust. Without measuring — that's the fun part, not measuring — slowly pour a little less than half of the bottle of caramel evenly over the apples. Put the pie shell in the freezer for 30 minutes to firm up the apples and caramel. When you do this, put the ice cream in the refrigerator to soften it. After 30 minutes, spoon the softened ice cream over the apples, pressing it down and smoothing it out with the back of a fork. Now pour as much of the remaining caramel over the ice cream as you like. Sprinkle the nuts over the top of the pie, and then put the pie back in the freezer for 1 hour to firm it up. Slice and serve.

Ice Cream Pumpkin Pie

1 quart vanilla ice cream, softened
1 (9 inch) pastry shell, baked
1 cup canned or cooked pumpkin
¾ cup sugar
½ teaspoon ground cinnamon
½ teaspoon salt
1 dash ground nutmeg
1 cup whipping cream, whipped

Syrup:
½ cup packed brown sugar
¼ cup water
¼ cup dark corn syrup

¼ teaspoon vanilla extract
⅛ teaspoon almond extract

Spread ice cream into pastry shell. Cover and freeze until firm. In a bowl, combine pumpkin, sugar, cinnamon, salt and nutmeg; fold in whipped cream. Pour evenly over ice cream; cover and freeze until firm. For syrup, combine brown sugar, water and corn syrup in saucepan; bring to a boil. Boil for 4 to 5 minutes, stirring often. Cool; stir in extracts. Drizzle over pie.

Lemonade Ice Cream Pie

1 pint vanilla ice cream, slightly softened
1 (6 ounce) can Frozen Lemonade, thawed
1 container (8 ounce size) Cool Whip
3 drops Yellow Food Coloring
1 graham cracker crust

Blend the ice cream, lemonade, Cool Whip and yellow food coloring with an electric mixer until smooth. Pour into graham cracker crust and freeze. Keep leftovers in freezer. This is a super easy recipe for children to make this summer!

Index

A

Appetizers & Snacks

B

Beverages

Breads

D

E

Entrees

S

Soups, Salads & Sides

"Great Grandma Don't You Remember Me?"

Great Grandma Margaret with Jack Louis December 2001

This poem was written for Jack Louis Holthaus
June 11, 2006
After Great Grandma's 90th Birthday Party
(Sadly, she didn't recognize him......)

My Great Grandma's name is Margaret
Her eyes are clear and blue,
She smiles and looks right at me,
And says "Do I know you?"

I tell her "My name is Jack Louis"
She says "Oh that's nice, Louis was my husbands' name."
I tell her Great Grandpa Louie is in Heaven now.
She says she's glad I came.

I remind her she held me as a baby.
That she bought my first outfit of blue.
"Great Grandma don't you remember?
It had a little choo-choo."

"Remember you held me on your lap when I was only three.
My legs would dangle down the chair
Great Grandma don't you remember me??
Great Grandma, don't you care?"

Then Great Grandma just smiled and laughed
She liked to hear my stories
But when I asked her if she knew my name
She stared out at the morning glories.

"Great Grandma" I tried again "I know
you will remember this"
One day I could reach up
And touch your shoulders with both my feet on the floor.
You bent down and gave me a kiss
And I said "One more, one more!"

I started to get worried as she gave me a blank stare
"Great Grandma don't you remember me?"
"I'd know YOU anywhere!"

My lips started to tremble and my eyes filled with tears,
My mother came to hold me and asked
"Jack what do you fear?"

"Great Grandma doesn't know me" I said
"And I love her so
She doesn't remember who I am
Maybe I should go."

My mom replied "Is that what you really think she wants?
To be left alone?
Don't you think she's lonely?
Here in the nursing home?"

"Jack, you tell her funny stories
I'm sure she loves to hear
You help her to know a time
When her mind was clear."

"Oh, I didn't know" I said
I thought she'd forgotten me on purpose."
"I thought she didn't love me anymore."
"Never" my mother said
And she's was very serious.

"Jack, now that you are eight years old"
You can understand
Your Great Grandma will always love you
In the best way that she can."

"It is you who must now remember
And keep her stories alive
Tell her all the good she's done for you.
Remember her kind eyes."

I hugged my mom then I gave my Great Grandma a big kiss
She is now 90 years old
And though sometimes she forgets
In her heart she really loves me,

I MUST remember this.

Ben Michael, Great Grandma and Jack Louis Summer 2000

Zoë Rae and Great Grandma at Zoë's First Communion 2000

Great Grandma with all of her Holthaus great grandchildren
Jack, Emily, Blake, Great Grandma, Zoë, Ben and a very upset Jared

About the Author

Columnist Sandy Holthaus lives on a farm in rural South Haven, Minnesota with her husband Mike and their children Zoë, Jack and Ben yet her heart remains on the North Shore of Lake Superior where she was raised by her parents, Art and LaVonne Anderson of Schroeder. She enjoys writing about her childhood and mixes memories with delicious helpings of home-style recipes.

You can send Sandy an e-mail of your thoughts and comments at: **sandyisms@mail.com**

Life Motto:
Just because I laugh a lot, doesn't mean my life is easy. Just because I have a smile on my face every day, doesn't mean that something is not bothering me. It's just that I choose to move on from the negative in my life and keep my head up instead of dwelling on the past.
~ Wise Author Unknown